BEYOND SELF-CARE POTATO CHIPS

Choosing Nourishing Self-Care in a Quick-Fix Culture

AMBER WARDELL, PhD
Psychology Today contributor and TikTok's @sensible_amber

Health Communications, Inc.
Boca Raton, Florida

www.hcibooks.com

Library of Congress Cataloging-in-Publication Data
is available through the Library of Congress

ISBN-13: 978-07573-2522-9 (Paperback)
ISBN-10: 007573-2522-X (Paperback)
ISBN-13: 978-07573-2523-6 (ePub)
ISBN-10: 07573-2523-8 (ePub)

Publisher: Health Communications, Inc.
301 Crawford Boulevard, Suite 200
Boca Raton, FL 33432-3762

Cover, interior design, and formatting by Larissa Hise Henoch.

For Charlie.

The rest of the books will be for the kids.

This one is for you.

Contents

Dear Reader,

As I share my journey of embracing nourishing self-care, I want to be sensitive toward the social dynamics at play. Conversations surrounding self-care cannot be divorced from the broader structures of rampant consumerism, patriarchy, ableism, and prejudice that shape our society. These systems profoundly influence our understanding of self-care, and it is crucial that we confront their impact head-on.

Self-care, in its truest form, should be inclusive and accessible to all. But this is an ideal—an ideal that has not yet been realized. Self-care, in many ways, remains a privilege rather than a right. It is mostly accessible only to those who have material wealth and resources, who are physically and mentally healthy, and who have an abundance of our most limited human resource: time. Sadly, much of the self-care culture we see in media and online depicts a kind of leisure-class privilege that is simply unreachable by the majority of us. By acknowledging this, we take the first step toward dismantling these structures and working toward a more equitable understanding and practice of self-care.

This book pushes against toxic, consumeristic self-care culture that avails itself primarily to the most privileged among us. It emphasizes the kind of real self-care that is accessible to us all because it exists within us all. However, it's important to address up front that when it comes to the intersection of self-care and systems of oppression, my perspective is inherently limited. As a woman, I have firsthand experience of how consumerism, sexism, and misogyny constrain our ability to engage in true self-care. I address many of those constraints head-on in this book. But as an able-bodied white woman with a certain degree of class privilege, I have not lived the experiences necessary to fully comprehend the nuances and depths of how racial issues, poverty, disability, and other challenges may impact self-care. Although I have made every effort to present self-care in a way that is accessible to all, my insights inevitably have been filtered through my own lived experiences and reflect my lack of perspective on how self-care is experienced and expressed in communities outside my own.

I invite you to approach this book as a starting point, as an invitation to delve deeper into the complexities of self-care. Engage critically, challenge existing narratives, and actively seek out diverse perspectives. By doing so, we can collectively foster a more inclusive, intersectional, and compassionate understanding of self-care that recognizes and confronts the systems that perpetuate inequality.

—Amber

Preface

We all know the feeling. Hunger strikes at precisely the wrong time, and you have no choice but to do something about it. You're exhausted, grouchy, and in a hurry, and the thought of preparing a nutritious snack sounds like more trouble than it's worth. So, you take the easy route and dig a grease-covered bag of potato chips out of the pantry instead. You rip open the bag and before you know it, your desire for another handful of savory goodness leaves you with only the crumbly bits at the bottom of the bag.

You look at your salt- and oil-covered fingertips—evidence that you did, in fact, just eat—and can't understand why you don't feel full. You consider grabbing another snack, but after tallying up the calories you just inhaled, you think better of it. Besides, break's over anyway. The things that keep you overworked and underwhelmed still need to be done. *Maybe next time*, you think. Next time, you'll eat something that satisfies.

A woman's life is filled with these potato chip moments. We have cravings that need to be satisfied, but satisfaction feels too far away to grasp. We hunger for self-care. We thirst for alone time, taking on new hobbies, and learning new things. We wonder if it's time to do something about our mental health. But life is busy with many demands, and who has time for self-care when so many other important things need to be done? We settle for the self-care equivalent of potato chips. We choose things that are quick and easy but that will not, and cannot, fulfill. As mothers, we count showers and trips to the grocery store as self-care and wonder why we still feel the constant urge to escape our kids. As working women, we take on more demands than we can handle and call it *ambition*, then we wonder why we're burned out. As wives and partners, we settle for the bare minimum because "at least he doesn't cheat" and wonder where our sex drive went. We settle for potato chips here and there and tell ourselves that it's enough, but we never feel full.

Much of my time in therapy has focused on my tendency to fill up on the things that can't nourish: people-pleasing, lacking healthy boundaries, making myself small so other people can feel big. These things are as temporarily satisfying, and vexingly useless, as potato chips. They are behaviors that feel like self-care because they elicit nice things like kindness, acceptance, and approval from others, but just like potato chips, they can't *really* fulfill. The kindness they earn comes with strings attached; the acceptance and approval come with the condition that we keep sacrificing ourselves or be unceremoniously discarded. They keep us reaching desperately back into the bag for more, hoping to one day get full.

My therapist told me that these practices are like self-care potato chips, and I've thought of nothing else since. It's hard to get full eating potato chips. You have to eat fistfuls of them to feel any measure of satisfaction. In the same way, self-care that doesn't involve caring deeply and intimately about *your essential self* will never feel satisfying. When I finally understood this fundamental truth, it completely changed my relationship with self-care. I found real nourishment—the abiding kind that lasts. I found a well of joy that I didn't know existed, and I learned to draw from it whenever I want. I am finally, and abundantly, full.

You can do the same. It takes some work, and some unlearning of the patriarchal garbage that has been dumped on us for far too long, but it can be done. All I ask of you is to put down the potato chips.

It sounds so easy. Yet, my own life has shown that it can be so frustratingly hard. How do we learn to reach for something more fulfilling when, since childhood, we have been told that potato chips are all we deserve? The training we receive as girls is so hard to shake. We spend our childhoods in a world that seems to adore and despise us at the same time. We see images of ourselves, half naked and tanned, everywhere we look. Perfect bodies. Perfect boyfriends. Perfect lives. We are told that all of this is attainable because being a woman is easy and beautiful. Just drink this calorie-free, fat-free, flavor-free tea and it can all be yours. Everything is in reach, provided that we reach for the right things. Reach for impractical underwear that digs into places it doesn't belong? You've got it! Reach for a husband and two-and-a-half kids in whom you can invest all your divine, feminine, and finite energy while you slowly, invisibly disappear? Why, yes, my pretty. You can have that, too. You can have it all. The world at your perfectly manicured fingertips.

But try reaching for the things that the contemptible "they" say we shouldn't, and watch how the world shrinks. We ask for things like a harassment-free workplace, and they call us uptight. We suggest that getting married and becoming stay-at-home moms might not be the right path for us, and they call us crazy cat ladies. And when we do choose marriage and motherhood but dare to suggest that those familial roles don't fulfill our hungry and thirsty souls—that maybe a happy life requires something more—they slap labels on us like ungrateful wives. Shameful mothers. Godless feminists.

We live in a world that wasn't designed with us in mind. Our place in society, and our contribution to it, was concocted mainly by men: white, Christian men, to be exact. Those men envisioned a world in which women were meant to serve, to be submissive to their husbands, devoted to their children, and eager to be meek, selfless, and charitable. We were told at the dinner table and from the pulpit that this is the life that good, godly women want for themselves. Women who wanted anything different were harlots, or maybe even witches.

That is not to say that women who want traditional, gender-based roles are bad. Some of the most important women in my life have wanted those things, and I love them for it.

My point is that I want *more* than that. I want to be selfish. I want to feel entitled to rest, to kick my feet up at the end of the day and not think about all the ways I could have done better. I want as much esteem and respect as a mediocre man without having to be ten times as good as him for people to think I deserve it. The world was just not made for women who want those things.

I do think that we have come a long way in changing the world for women like us—the women who hunger and thirst for more than what the world says should fill us up. We still have a long way to go, but I'm proud of what we have accomplished so far. That said, those of us who grew up in a world that told us not to reach may have a hard time remembering how it's done.

I want this book to teach you how to reach again, how to reach for the things that satisfy you deep, deep down, not for the potato chips you've been told should be enough. You used to know how, before it was trained out of you. The little girl inside you still knows. We just have to make her feel safe enough to try.

To do that, we're going to have to dig some truth trenches—some barriers that create space between ourselves and the lies that society loves to tell us. Building a truth trench is like digging a canal in the ground all the way around you. Inside this trench, you plant seeds of truth. These truths are deeply personal and will vary for everyone, but they consist of things like *I am allowed to rest. I deserve to make my needs a priority. I cannot pour from an empty cup*. With time, the truths in our truth trench begin to grow and form a barrier through which the lies of the world have to pass. Cleansed and refined by truth, the lies lose their power.

I want this book to be a truth trench. It will take time for you to learn how to plant your own truth trenches so, for now, I'd like to let you borrow mine. I've spent many hours in therapy building these trenches, these great, shimmering truths that have removed the shame and fear that stopped me from reaching.

I am a storyteller, a theater kid at heart, and telling stories is the best way I know how to make complex conversations accessible and relatable to everyone. So, you're about to hear a lot of stories about my life. Things about my marriage, my kids, my job, my family dynamics, and my mental health. Each of these things—the beautiful, the sparkling, the sad, and the chaotic—has taught me something about what it means to reach—what it means to stop settling for potato chips—and to instead grasp for the things that truly fulfill.

Through these stories, you'll learn that I am a woman filled with contradictions. I am a progressive feminist who hailed from a staunchly Christian, conservative family with whom I have a loving and fulfilling relationship. I'm a Christian myself, who holds on to my faith while being unapologetically outspoken about the harms of the American Christian church. I'm a bisexual woman in a committed heterosexual marriage, being essentially straight-passing while struggling to find my place in the LGBTQIA community. I am a neurotypical woman living in a household full of neurodiverse people, learning how different and yet how strikingly similar our brains are. I'm also a businesswoman with a doctorate degree who has deep-seated passion for my career, yet still clings to some traditional ideas about my role in my family.

Amid all these contradictions, I have learned how to maintain unity within myself and harmony with the people around me. And this is what I feel is the biggest truth trench of all: Self-care, in its proper context, flows outward. It starts from within and blossoms out to our romantic, familial, professional, and platonic relationships. It teaches us how to love ourselves well, and then it shows us how to maintain healthy relationships with the people we desire to keep in our lives, how to let go of the people we don't, and how to know the difference between the two.

Throughout this book, I'm also going to share interesting principles and tidbits from cognitive psychology, my second love. Together, we are going to create truth trenches—ones that speak the truth about who you are as a person who has worth, who deserves to be full. We're going to show that little girl deep inside that she can reach again. And this time, when she reaches, it won't be for potato chips.

SECTION I
Breakfast in Bed:
Self-Care in Marriage and Relationships

Chapter One

Apartment(s)

Keys trembling in my hand, I stood at the threshold of my new apartment. Years spent white-knuckling my marriage had left me broken and exhausted, zapped of whatever fight I thought would get us through it. I couldn't believe it had come to this.

My perfect, sparkling marriage of seven years had fallen apart. I had lost myself. And the dreams to which I had clung so tightly had slipped entirely through my fingers. I was miserable, my kids were miserable, and although my husband, Charlie, insisted that he was happy and wanted to try to fix our broken marriage, I could see that he was miserable, too.

There were many culprits in the demise of our marriage. There was the postpartum depression that never seemed to fully let go, even years after the kids were no longer babies. There was Charlie's Crohn's disease—a debilitating illness that had robbed him of his dignity and bodily autonomy. There was his dependence on the medications that kept the worst of his symptoms at bay but that also made him irritable, narcoleptic, and depressed.

We argued over money. We argued over the kids. We argued over the unfair division of labor and my resentment over being the default parent, the default household manager, the default wiper of butts and maker of meals.

We argued about sex. Charlie wondered why we didn't do it as much as we used to, and I wondered *where in the hell* I was supposed to find my sex drive when I was drowning in a sea of chores, and kids, and struggling to invigorate my burgeoning business that was in its infancy and needed my constant attention.

Maybe it was buried somewhere in the mountain of dirty laundry piling up in our closet. Maybe if he would do a load of it himself, he would find my sex drive tucked away in there like money hidden among the pages of a long-forgotten book.

But he wouldn't do that. So there it stayed.

These things take a toll, even in the strongest relationships.

Gradually, I watched the resentment build and our perfect marriage begin to crumble. We went through years of struggle and trauma and attempts to mend things that were far too broken. I was exhausted and just so damn angry. There was never any physical damage, but the mental, emotional, and spiritual damage that I'd sustained in that marriage had taken a significant toll on me. And to be honest, I think that's all I want to say about that. Some things are just too hard to revisit, even after years of healing.

In November 2021, I told Charlie that I wanted a separation. My children were still so small, only five and three years old at the time. Even though we had tried to protect them from the worst of our deteriorating relationship, they knew things hadn't been right in a very long time. They were smart and intuitive, even at their young age, and we could see that the knowledge of our constant fighting was weighing heavily on them. In the early years of our marriage, we had promised that we would stay together for the children no matter what. But making promises like that, as we learned, is easy when you haven't seen how bad things can actually get. In an effort to protect our children from our own brokenness while we decided if our marriage was salvageable, we chose to live separately and split custody of the children equally. I would enjoy the kids for one week, then Charlie would enjoy them the next week, and this was how we would live until we decided to reconcile or divorce.

I told Charlie that I wanted to be the one to move out; our house just held too many difficult memories for me, and I didn't believe I could heal while I was there. So, I set about the heartbreaking work of finding a place to do my healing away from the memories that haunted me.

A few weeks later, there I was. Standing outside my new apartment, breathless. Exhilarated to finally get to recover and heal. Grief-stricken by what I had to give up to do it.

I wasn't sure what to expect, joy or despair, when I walked through that door for the first time. I guess the honest answer is that it was both—and neither—maybe the two mixed together and then diluted in a solution called *fear of the unknown*.

What I did know for certain as I looked around the barren, echoey living room that wouldn't be filled with furniture until the next day was that life was about to be beautifully, if frightfully, different.

I had spent years living my life for my family. I was proud of that, happy that I had given all of myself to the people in my care. But the damage this had done to my essential self, to the *me* I had once loved and protected, was substantial. I wasn't sure if I wanted to reconcile my marriage, or instead to learn how to be alone, but I did know that the only way to find out was to begin connecting with that self again, finding out what she needs in her innermost parts, and getting those things for her.

The first thing I did was begin reading. I devoured self-help books like they were my last meal. I read impressive women like Brené Brown and Glennon Doyle. I read ancient wisdom of the Dalai Lama and Jesus Christ. I found comfort in these faithful friends who told me every day that I was enough. I was capable of finding happiness for myself. I could create a life that brought joy. Satisfaction, even.

I found comfort in these faithful friends who told me every day that I was enough. I was capable of finding happiness for myself. I could create a life that brought joy. Satisfaction, even.

I journaled every day. I wrote down every sad, beautiful, and chaotic thought that came to my mind. I read my entries to my therapist each week, and we worked through them all.

On the weeks I didn't have my kids, I devoted myself to doing things that made me happy. I taught myself how to bake. I had friends over for dinner and drinks. Strolled the aisles of Barnes and Noble for hours. Started going to the gym regularly. I enjoyed the very undervalued privilege of being able to come and go as I pleased with no one to answer to but myself. I had forgotten what a joy kidless grocery shopping could be.

For the first time since becoming a mom, I was beginning to feel like my old self again. And this got me wondering, *When did I lose her? When did I forget how to make myself a priority in my own life?*

When did the little girl inside stop reaching?

One night, while alone in my new apartment and pondering these things, something inside me that had been threatening to break for years finally splintered, then shattered. Then and there, I made a commitment to finding out where that girl went and how to bring her back. I wanted to live in a world that gave me all the things I needed and deserved, and maybe that had to begin with me. I decided I would take however long it took to figure out how to stand up for myself, to speak my needs. I would learn to stop shrinking and making myself small to make room for other people.

I wanted to live in a world that gave me all the things I needed and deserved, and maybe that had to begin with me. I decided I would take however long it took to figure out how to stand up for myself, to speak my needs. I would learn to stop shrinking and making myself small to make room for other people.

My weekly therapy sessions became less about reexamining the past and more about the practical matters of taking care of myself in the present. A word that came up in almost every session was *freedom*. As we dove deeper into that word, I found that it always seemed to produce the imagery of a bird in a cage.

"What do you think that symbolizes?" my therapist had asked.

"I am the bird," I explained. "I love my life, but I never get to fly. I can see what's out there beyond the cage. I just can't get to it."

He asked me a question that still haunts me. "Amber, is the cage locked? Or is it just closed?" He blinked, waiting for me to comprehend. "What I mean to say is, maybe if you would dare to push on the door a bit, you'd find that the only one keeping you in there is you."

What if the cage was a trap of my own making, forged by people-pleasing and self-neglect? A trap made by me that other people had learned to use to their own advantage? What if self-care meant pushing the door open and *insisting* on being free? Freedom would come from stepping into my power and, for the first time in years, putting myself first.

I started small, making myself a priority in the low-stakes areas of my life. Then, with practice, I worked my way up to the stuff with higher stakes.

It began with strangers and acquaintances. I stopped apologizing when someone stepped on *my* foot. I started giving firm *noes* instead of half-hearted *yeses*. I learned to stop overexplaining myself. Though it was hard, I gradually learned to stop sacrificing my peace at the altar of politeness.

These little victories gave me the confidence to start prioritizing myself in bigger ways. I started setting boundaries with family members and cutting ties with friends who were unhealthy for me. I began the hard work of establishing some needed boundaries with my kids, who were well behaved but who had also learned how to walk all over me.

In fits and starts, I was learning how to show up for myself the way I had always needed to. I was finally feeling fulfilled, joyful, and satisfied with my life. As my relationship with myself and my loved ones healed, I began thinking about the one relationship that was still broken. It had been almost six months since the first time I turned the key in my new apartment. As busy as I had been during that time, Charlie had been busy, too. He had been in therapy; he had gotten his depression under control. We had gone on a few dates together during our separation and I could see that he was evolving just like I was. I missed him.

Gradually, we began discussing what reconciling would look like. We took it slow, but it still seemed to happen breathtakingly fast. I was nervous. This was the one relationship in which I had lost myself the most—the Petri dish from which my self-neglect had begun to grow. It would be terrifyingly easy to fall back into old routines.

But I had been practicing. If there was anything I had learned over the course of my solo self-care journey, it was that strict boundaries and clear communication have a magic about them. I had watched myself become a better person, and inexplicably, the people around me were becoming better people, too. If the magic could happen with them, it was worth giving it a try with Charlie.

If there was anything I had learned over the course of my solo self-care journey, it was that strict boundaries and clear communication have a magic about them.

I will not go back into a cage.

Every conversation with him went back to that. There were many things I would do to save our marriage and make it healthy again, but the cage was not one of them. Putting all my hard work to practice, I explained to Charlie what Not Going Back into the Cage would look like in our marriage going forward. There would be balance and equity. There would be open communication, a willingness to share and receive feedback about our satisfaction in the marriage. He would have to become more observant and proactive regarding household and childcare responsibilities, and we would both do better about establishing healthy boundaries with outside influences like work, family, and friends, since even these objectively good things can do damage when there are no limits around them.

Most importantly, I would no longer be making my needs small. If we were going to start over, I wouldn't allow myself to be sustained on self-care potato chips. I would reach, always, for freedom and fullness.

Charlie agreed to the terms, and within a few short weeks we had broken the lease on my little apartment. We also packed up our home in the suburbs and got it ready for sale. We decided that a new start deserved a new home, one that wasn't heavy with memories of times we would rather forget. So, we signed a lease on a trendy loft apartment in the city. We were ready to start our new life together. The last thing to do was pack up my apartment.

When we loaded the last box of my things onto the U-Haul, I took one final look around the apartment that had been my haven. I felt Charlie's arm slip around me, and he kissed my temple. This place had done its job. It had given me a place to hide, to lick my wounds and focus on healing. In the end, it had brought me back to the very thing I was running from. Tucked away behind those walls, I learned how to take care of myself again. I was happy, healed, and whole and finally repaired enough to try it all again. This time, making myself a priority. Insisting on it.

Looking back, I wish I didn't need to uproot my life and move out of my home in order to arrive at this place. But, to be honest, I don't think I had any other choice. Sometimes, the hurt and the brokenness are so deep that you have to go somewhere to clear your mind, lick your wounds, and truly heal.

Sometimes, the hurt and the brokenness are so deep that you have to go somewhere to clear your mind, lick your wounds, and truly heal.

We all have different struggles, different things in our lives that keep us reaching for the potato chips of self-care instead of the things we truly need to be nourished and fulfilled. Maybe you don't need to move out or start your life over like I did, whether permanently or for a time, or maybe you do. My hope for you is that whatever that thing is that you need in order to begin the journey of true self-care, you will get it for yourself. You will forcefully, unapologetically, *bombastically* seek out what you need to put down the potato chips and reach for fulfillment.

I know that's scary.

It scared me, too.

But it's actually pretty easy once you master a few important principles. It's my deepest wish that this book will impart those principles to you and show you how to carry them out. Once you have tasted the richness, the absolute deliciousness that life has to offer when you take care of yourself the way you truly deserve, you'll never settle for potato chips again.

Cultivate Your Truth Trench

- **Being honest with yourself takes courage.** You will find yourself in situations that are bad for your mental health and well-being. You owe it to yourself to be honest about that and to be brave enough to make necessary changes, even if it's difficult.
- **People-pleasing is self-neglect.** Somewhere along the way, someone (maybe many someones) taught you that you come second. You deserve to come first. If not with anyone else, at least with yourself. This can be difficult when you have people who depend on you, but you cannot show up best for those people when you aren't taking care of yourself.
- **Small, incremental steps give you the confidence to take the bigger ones.** Start small by asserting yourself in low-stakes situations, then gradually work your way up to more significant changes and boundary settings.
- **You don't belong in cages.** Have you let yourself be put in cages made by others, or even by your own hand? If you dared to push the door open, what might you find in the world beyond the cage? It is time to let yourself out of the cage and step into true and fulfilling freedom. Self-care is the daring business of breaking bars and chains.

Chapter Two
Maslow

I often think about how strange it is that most of the love stories we see as little girls end at what's actually the beginning. Cinderella marries the prince while her wicked stepsisters watch in dismay, and the newly betrothed couple lives happily ever after. Belle, and Ariel, and Briar Rose, and an unending list of broken girls find the man who will fix them, and they live. Happily. Ever. Godforsaken. After.

The end.

Don't get me wrong; I love a happy ending. There is enough misery in the world, and I don't suppose it's a bad thing for little girls to see that love, harmony, and an easy life are possible. But I do wonder what kinds of self-limiting distortions of romance we are teaching our children with these stories that end with a vague and infinite *happy*. Is that the goal? Just . . . fall in love and expect the rest of your days to be filled with fancy balls and carriage rides? Don't mind me, but I'd like to see some of these fairy-tale marriages in a few years when life has settled into the disenchanted and familiar routine. What happens then?

We teach our little girls that love is enough, but research on human motivation and needs tells us a much different story. In

1943, a psychologist named Abraham Maslow published his first paper on the hierarchy of needs that explained how our needs evolve over time. Maslow differentiated between what he called *deficiency needs* and *growth needs*. Our basic human needs like food, shelter, safety, and even love make up the deficiency needs. As their name implies, they are needs that arise when we lack something. A lack of food gives rise to hunger, so we need to find nourishment. A lack of employment gives rise to instability, so we need to find a job. And, circling back to our blessed princesses, a lack of love gives rise to loneliness and gloom, so we need to find a mate. Every one of the deficiency needs shows us what's missing and drives us toward acquiring it.

There is only one *growth* need in Maslow's original model, and it is called self-actualization. Self-actualization is about evolving to our highest potential. It is about transcendence. For many, that can look like finding our calling—the thing that everyone looking on says, "She's doing what she was born to do." Do you remember Prince's 2007 Super Bowl performance? The one where he sang "Purple Rain" in an actual rainstorm? Many people have said that it was the best Super Bowl performance of all time, the best show of Prince's career, and a glittering example of a person doing what they were born to do.

But not everyone's version of self-actualization will be as flashy as that. For some, self-actualization can look like becoming the best parent they can be, landing their dream job, or simply learning to love themselves. No matter what our own brand of self-actualization might look like, Maslow was clear about one thing: True love is not our highest calling, no matter what the fairy tales say. Self-actualization, discovering what we were born to do and doing it, is the only thing that will lead us to our fullest potential. Why does society insist on telling little girls that finding love is the last stop on the road to fulfillment? According to Maslow, love is just a stepping stone.

Self-actualization, discovering what we were born to do and doing it, is the only thing that will lead us to our fullest potential.

When love is sincere, it can be the springboard from which to launch ourselves toward reaching the highest versions of ourselves. But love is the vehicle, not the destination. If our culture lets little girls believe that love is the ultimate goal, it shouldn't be surprising that, when we become young women, we find ourselves disillusioned and bored once the initial romance of love wears off. We are, and have always been, destined for something more. We know it in our hearts, and our souls cry out for it. But as long as we believe that simply finding love is supposed to satisfy and fulfill, we will never know to reach for more.

To be honest, sometimes I think that was the point.

Women who demand more than love from their romantic partners are deemed dangerous and demanding. They won't settle for relationships that define the wedding day as the pinnacle of happiness. Instead, they expect partners who actively enrich and support them, and who encourage them to reach for the highest form of self-actualization possible. They won't commit to a relationship until they find that kind of partner. And once they do commit, they will expect their partner to maintain that level of support or risk being left in the dust. This is a threat to the patriarchal, heteronormative establishment of marriage and relationships that prioritizes the ease and comfort of men over that of women—the one that allows them to provide the bare minimum and call us nags for wanting more—therefore, the fairy tales must end at happily ever after.

When I made the decision to reconcile my marriage, I knew that from then on, I would make self-actualization my priority. I was putting away the self-limiting belief that I could get full on potato chips in the form of romance and "true love" and would instead dive into the hearty goodness of discovering my highest self. I could do it on my own, but I chose to believe that it could be done better with a supportive partner by my side. And in order for us to succeed, I would need to teach Charlie how to be that partner for me.

We had many conversations about what this meant as we began the process of weaving our lives back together after the separation. The first step was identifying what self-actualization actually looked like for me. It took some time to really understand my own self-actualization needs and then to figure out how to communicate them to Charlie. When I finally sorted it all out, the list of self-actualization needs that I shared with him looked like this:

- I love being with the children, but my career is important to me, and I need your support in pursuing it.
- We are better together when we are both in therapy, and I would like for us to make that a priority.
- I love Jesus, but I think I have too much religious trauma to go back to church. I need to work through some things, and I need you to understand.
- My identity as a bisexual woman is important to me, but I spent years hiding that part of myself from the world. I have a need to be connected to the LGBTQ community, and I want your support.
- I need you to support my hobbies, encourage my relationships with my friends, and give me guilt-free alone time so that I can center and reset.

There was such a relief in communicating this list to Charlie. I knew I had a long way to go before I felt self-actualized in all those areas, but if he could commit to supporting me in each of these things, maybe I could get there faster and with less of a struggle. It has been an interesting road paved with lots of learning on both of our parts. It was hard to look him in the eyes and say, "I need you to honor these needs I have, or else I can't be in a relationship with you."

Like so many of us, I've been conditioned to believe that clearly saying what I need and setting a boundary that comes with consequences is mean. Selfish, even. I've also had the religious upbringing that says that marriage is forever, and love is unconditional. *How do I put conditions around a relationship that is meant to have none?*

If you have had the same conditioning as me, and I'm betting you have, here's what I need you to know:

- Self-care is not selfish.
- Saying what you need is not mean.
- Your love is allowed to have conditions and limits.

So many of us have come to believe that we are selfish for insisting that our needs are met or that we are disgraceful for walking away from our marriages when they don't meet our expectations. These beliefs stop us from reaching for what we need and deserve. The truth trench I'd like to dig for you right now, which I hope you will cultivate on your own, is that there is no shame in getting your needs met. You have permission to decide that love for the sake of love is not enough, that your happily ever after requires more effort than that. You are not obligated to give unconditional love to someone who does not return it to you.

If there is any part of you that isn't convinced that prioritizing yourself, reaching for the sustaining goodness of self-actualization instead of accepting *just love* as your happily ever after, I need you to really hear me: the beautiful, sparkling, and breathtaking paradox of putting yourself first is that in so doing, you become a better partner yourself.

The beautiful, sparkling, and breathtaking paradox of putting yourself first is that, in so doing, you become a better partner yourself.

In sharing what I needed to reach my highest self and fullest potential with my husband, I found him stepping up in ways I couldn't have imagined. He learned me. It was as if he was seeing me in my true, essential nature for the first time. He began making an effort to support me in my self-actualization, and he gets better at it every day.

As I feel my husband's support give me the gentle leg up that pushes me closer to self-actualization, I find myself happy, satisfied, and fulfilled. That fulfillment pours outward, onto my husband and my children. No longer exhausted and overwhelmed by the frustration of not having my needs met, I now have the resources and energy to push Charlie toward his highest potential. Although my children are still small, I can already see glimmers of what their highest potential may be, and I am working to foster and encourage their pursuit of it. I am learning that I always wanted to show up for my family this way.

I just couldn't do it from inside the cage.

Cultivate Your Truth Trench

- **The idea of fairy-tale love is useless.** Life is not a fairy tale, no matter what the Disney movies want us to believe. The love we see in fairy tales is not only unrealistic and unsustainable, it also sets us up for disappointment as we navigate relationships in the real world. Sensible self-care is about having proper expectations about what purpose love is supposed to serve. Spoiler: you are meant to have so much more than romance.
- **Love is the journey, not the destination.** Self-actualization is the true path to fulfillment. Love is not the ultimate goal but rather a vehicle for personal growth and transcendence. Anyone who tells you that "true love" is the happily ever after is asking you to settle for less than you deserve.
- **Women who know what they deserve are dangerous.** Society conditions women to accept the bare minimum from their partners and calls them "nags" if they ask for more. It's time for you to become such a dangerous woman. Self-care is challenging norms that tell you to be happy with what you get and insisting instead on getting what you deserve.
- **Your love should come with conditions.** Romantic partners should enrich your life, just as you enrich theirs. Working together to meet each other's highest needs allows you to become your most fulfilled, authentic selves. You are allowed to say, "I will not stay in a relationship where my needs go unfulfilled."

Chapter Three

The Core of the Matter

I'm about to talk about sex.

When did I start feeling like I need to give a trigger warning before talking about it? Sex used to be such an exciting word—one filled with longing, anticipation, hunger. But upon entering my late thirties and being married almost a decade, I found that the word had lost some of its sparkle. For a while, the sex had lost its sparkle, too. In fact, it was one of the causes of our separation. Sex had become a part of the cage.

When Charlie and I chose to reconcile, I found sex to be a topic of conversation we had to revisit often. There was no future of a happy and successful marriage that didn't include our addressing some pretty serious stuff about our sex life. What began as a conversation about sex turned into a broader and much more useful conversation about what we *actually* need. Spoiler alert—it goes deeper than sex.

The act of sex itself had never been a problem for us. Our sex life was curious and spontaneous. It could be romantic, or playful, or carnal. In the beginning, untainted by the problems that settled into our marriage later on, it was perfect.

But as time marched forward and children were born, exhaustion set in, conversation broke down, and sex became a major obstacle for us both. It was happening less frequently. When it did happen, it was more like a business transaction. A quick handshake. Although I once looked forward to our bedtime escapades, I found myself dreading them, counting how many days it had been since we last did it, and wondering how many more I could get away with until it became an argument. I was exhausted from years of being awakened all night by sleep-regressed kiddos who, as the years went on, never really shook their difficult sleeping habits. My body was worn down from twelve-hour days on my feet. I was only showering every three to five business days, so I wasn't feeling super great about my hygiene, either. Naturally, my interest in sex had begun to wane.

I loved Charlie, but I was tired. And he just couldn't see that. He felt rejected and unwanted, a feeling he has run away from since he was a boy. A lifetime spent wondering if he was lovable did a lot of damage to Charlie's self-worth. Sex with me was validation for him. A reassurance of my devotion. Without sex, he didn't know if he was loved. This self-doubt, this fear of being discarded, created a self-fulfilling prophecy in which he got the very rejection he feared. Because he was constantly seeking opportunities for sex—leering at me when I got out of the shower, groping me while I cooked dinner—I became frustrated and fed up. I rejected him over and over because I was exhausted, and smelly, and touched out.

Perhaps, if he had helped me with my exhaustion, and my smelliness, and my touched-out-edness, I would have had the energy and enthusiasm for sex. His all-too-frequent attempts at intimacy, and all-too-few attempts at helping me with the laundry, left me resentful and angry.

While we were separated, I insisted that Charlie go to therapy to address the rejection issues that were at the root of his sexual needs. In my own therapy sessions, I focused on the resentment I felt about our sex life and the imbalance of expectations in our relationship. It was there, in these separate therapy sessions, that we both began to understand the meaning of *core needs.*

Core needs are the foundation of our happiness and well-being. They are the things that we absolutely cannot live without if we intend to be satisfied in our lives and our relationships. Core needs are distinct from the smaller, peripheral needs that make us happy but that we could live without if we had to. If those peripheral needs are the potato chips, our core needs are the casserole.

Core needs are the foundation of our happiness and well-being. They are the things that we absolutely cannot live without if we intend to be satisfied in our lives and our relationships.

What Charlie and I discovered through therapy was that our sexual conflicts were the symptom of our unhappiness, not the source. We both had deeper, more significant core needs that were going unmet. Self-care in our relationship would be a journey of identifying those needs and finding ways to get them met.

Most of Charlie's core needs are about connection. He grew up with a father who abandoned him at a very young age and started a new family. His childhood years were spent striving for acceptance and approval in all the wrong places—a habit that followed him into adulthood. His life had become a relentless pursuit of belonging. And because he was socialized as a man in a misogynistic culture, he was taught that the greatest form of connection and belonging was sex with a woman. My lack of sexual interest made him feel worthless and abandoned.

As for me, the majority of my core needs are about freedom. I need independence, a sense of agency over myself and the world around me. Becoming a mom was the greatest joy of my life, but it came at a cost. I now had children to think of—children who, quite frankly, needed more of me than I felt able to give. Things as simple as going to the grocery store were now a multistep ordeal. I loved being with my kids, but I often longed for the carefree girl I used to be. I wasn't getting the support I needed from Charlie at home, and because of my many obligations, I had no time for myself. When I *did* find moments of solitude and rest, Charlie had an uncanny way of showing up and expecting intimacy. *Exuberant* intimacy.

I had none to give, so I had begun locking myself in the bathroom instead.

Charlie's lack of connection and my lack of freedom had put us on opposite sides of an infinite chasm. He felt like that little boy whose dad couldn't bother to love him, and I felt like a bird in a cage. We were *alone, together,* which somehow felt lonelier than being all alone. Our failure to understand and show compassion toward each other's core needs had led us down paths traveling in opposite directions, doomed to never intersect.

Going to individual therapy showed us that in order to address the issue of sex, we had to address the underlying core needs first. Slowly, gently, we began opening up to each other about those needs. Charlie had spoken to me in the past about his abandonment issues and fear of rejection, but I had never understood how deep those waters ran. I learned that he lives in a constant dread of the people he loves leaving him. Sex, in his mind, was never about the physical act itself. It was about what the sex *meant.* It meant love, acceptance, and connection. If he had my body, then that meant he had my heart, too. And that meant that everything was okay.

I explained to Charlie that his need for connection, especially when it came to sex, was too much for me. I needed control over my body to not feel like sex was the currency with which I bought time for myself, and I never had enough in my account to pay the tab. I needed him to help me with our shared responsibilities so that I could have the time and the freedom to do things for me, the way I did before the kids came along.

After laying these needs bare before each other, the next step was to settle the practical matters of meeting them.

My list was very pragmatic. It consisted of things that I needed Charlie to step up and help me with so that I could have time for myself, to be free. I didn't need sweet but useless romantic gestures like roses and candy. I needed fair and equitable labor with the kids and the house. And when the kids were in bed and the chores were done, I needed *guilt-free* time for myself. Most of all, I needed rest. Charlie committed to stepping up with the tasks we share, and he followed through on that commitment. Now, he draws baths for me in the evenings and sets out my book, a towel, a glass of water (or wine), and a candle for me. This is how he shows me that my core need for alone time matters to him.

Charlie's list was more emotional than practical. He said that if I would try to be more intimate in nonsexual ways with him, like kissing his forehead or holding hands from time to time, it would help him feel more secure. He wanted regular date nights on weekends for us to reconnect, and for us to make more time for each other on weekdays when possible. These things were easy to say yes to because I want them, too. And I am more able to give them to him when I am rested and recharged from having more support and, of course, my alone time.

Sometimes, things took a bit more negotiation. When two people have core needs that are so diametrically opposed—him stretching toward me for connection, and me stretching away for independence—you learn the delicate art of compromise. We had to learn how to show up for each other's core needs without sacrificing our own. It was hard work, but with a renewed commitment to creating a marriage that satisfies, we figured it out.

These days, we don't sweat the small stuff too much. We don't mind when we fail to meet each other's small day-to-day needs because our biggest, most foundational core needs are met. I'm also proud to say that our sex life is back and healthier than ever. But it was never really about the sex. It was about two people desperate to be seen and understood. It was about reaching beneath the surface and accessing the deeper need. Not the sex, but the connection. Not the chores, but the freedom.

But it was never really about the sex. It was about two people desperate to be seen and understood. It was about reaching beneath the surface and accessing the deeper need. Not the sex, but the connection. Not the chores, but the freedom.

We have learned what it means to practice self-care within the context of a marriage. Our lives are intertwined in almost every way. Because of that, there is no path to achieving my maximum potential for self-care that doesn't include my husband. I need him involved. I need him aware of what I need. I need him to be willing to work with me to meet my needs. In the same way, the only way for Charlie to reach his fullest potential is for me to do the same for him. By each of us committing to care for the other's core needs while not neglecting or sacrificing our own, we have learned that everything else is pretty easy. Satiated by the fulfilling casserole of tending to our core needs, we don't argue over potato chips anymore.

Are you and your spouse or partner showing up for each other's core needs? If you're being honest with yourselves, can you even name what they are? For many of us, as time goes by we begin to know *less* about our partner instead of more. It's a bewildering feeling to wake up one day in a marriage that doesn't make sense, fighting over things like sex that used to bring you joy. And I think we arrive in that place for two reasons: First, we lose touch with our own needs. Second, we lose interest in our partner's needs. We lose touch with those needs because we lose touch with ourselves and with each other.

Self-care in our marriages begins with embarking on a path of self-discovery. This journey involves not only understanding our own core needs but also recognizing how our needs intersect with our partner's. It requires open communication, active listening, and deep empathy (things we will discuss more in upcoming chapters), both for ourselves and our partners. This involves taking time for self-reflection, asking questions, and embracing our desires and vulnerabilities. It means creating an environment of trust within which we feel safe expressing what our core needs are, both to ourselves and to each other.

Through this process of self-care that prioritizes understanding each other's needs at the *deepest and most self-actualizing level,* we build bridges instead of cages.

Cultivate Your Truth Trench

- **You can't be satisfied without your core needs being met.** Take time to discover your core needs. Core needs are your bottom line. In romantic relationships, it is important that you both know your core needs, express them to each other, and do your best to meet those needs for yourself and your partner.
- **It's almost never about sex.** You and your partner have core needs and past experiences that influence your sex life and romantic satisfaction. Often, the sexual problems resolve on their own when the deeper issues are addressed. If you allow yourselves to deprioritize sex and focus on the core needs instead, you may be surprised how quickly your sexual connection sparks back to life.
- **Self-care lies at the intersections.** Your life and your partner's are inextricably intertwined. Your core needs matter, and so do theirs. In marriages and romantic partnerships, compromise and negotiation are necessary to balance opposing core needs, and to foster mutual understanding and fulfillment.
- **Build bridges, not cages.** Making space for trust and empathy creates an environment where you and your partner can feel safe expressing your core needs and supporting each other's growth and well-being. When you focus on intimately knowing your partner's needs as well as your own—developing a posture of curiosity toward those needs and how to fulfill them—you build bridges to connection instead of cages of loneliness.

Chapter Four

Mind Reader

It was well into January, and our Christmas tree was still standing stupidly in our living room. The Christmas spirit had evaporated weeks ago, and I was ready to reclaim my space, but Charlie seemed content to leave the tree up until next Christmas. I made a big show of taking down the other Christmas trimmings in hopes that he would take the hint.

He did, in fact, not take the hint.

I had mentally delegated the task of taking down the tree to him. *Why wasn't he doing the thing I had told him a thousand times in my head that he needed to do?* I was getting that helpless, fed-up feeling you get when you accidentally put on an itchy sweater and don't realize it until you're too far from home to change.

Something had to be done.

One morning, when I'd finally reached my limit, I began tearing the tree down as loudly and dramatically as I could. I made an unnecessary show of tripping over fallen strings of lights and swearing. What might have been accomplished in about fifteen minutes, I strung out for an additional thirty. *Where was my stupid husband?* I needed him to see how much of an inconvenience his failure to read my mind had caused me.

Didn't he understand that taking down the Christmas tree is a *husband* job? Didn't he see how much work I had already done to undress the house of all the Christmas crap, and that this was the *one thing* I wanted him to do? I had the distinct urge to give him a wedgie.

I stormed upstairs and threw myself a pity party instead.

This Christmas-tree thing was a triggering event for me. It represented years of feeling like I carried a heavier load, like my husband didn't notice or care what I needed. That kind of thing does something to a person, and old triggers die hard, even when healing and reconciliation have taken place.

I guess, somewhere along the way, I bought into an idea about romance that I shouldn't have. Maybe I got it from movies or young adult fiction novels from my youth, or maybe from the #Instaperfect marriages I got used to seeing on Instagram. It just seemed like everywhere I looked was the image of the "perfect" husband who knew every one of your needs before you could even speak them. What better way to feel loved than to be so intimately known by someone?

I wanted to feel loved. I wanted to feel known, seen, and understood. If Charlie could just show me that he was so in tune with my needs that he could meet them without me asking, then I would know he loved me. The Christmas tree was a loud, ridiculous symbol of my husband's obtuseness to my needs. He should have just known I wanted him to take it down.

There is a term for this way of thinking. You're going to hate it. The term is *passive immobility.* Yes, that's a real psychological term. And although it sounds like a bad case of constipation, it's actually the scientific name for expecting people to read your mind. I guess, now that I'm thinking about it, it is sort of like constipation. We have things bottled up that would feel a lot better if we released them, but for some reason we can't squeeze them out, no matter how uncomfortable they make us. We decide that maybe they'll pass on their own if we just stop thinking about them.

There is a certain type of person who is most likely to engage in passive immobility. Are you ready? You're going to hate this even more.

It's *anxious people.* That's right. Calling all anxious folks to the front of the class. Passive immobility tends to happen when we feel anxious, uncertain, or vulnerable within the context of the relationship. That anxiety creates a fear of expressing ourselves, so we stuff our needs down and hope that our partners will read our minds instead.

Passive immobility tends to happen when we feel anxious, uncertain, or vulnerable within the context of the relationship. That anxiety creates a fear of expressing ourselves, so we stuff our needs down and hope that our partners will read our minds instead.

The years I spent hoping my husband would listen to my needs and take action on them, and being let down instead, had certainly made me feel anxious. Too many times I had spoken my needs only to be ignored. Or worse, to be promised that what I needed would be taken care of, just to be let down again. It created in me an intense fear of stating my needs and wants. The disappointment was so bitter when I reached for help and got none that I decided the safer approach was just to not reach. But that didn't stop me from needing and wanting. I still needed and wanted; I'd just stopped asking.

No wonder I was so desperate for him to read my mind.

The problem with this desperation to be known and understood—to have my husband predict my needs before I've spoken them—is that, as you may have guessed, he's not very good at it. Nobody is. Expecting him to know what I need without me saying it is unfair to him and to me. What *is* fair is being brave enough to say what I need and to give him the opportunity to show up for me. The alternative is staying silent and leaving him only the opportunity to let me down.

I deserve to have my needs met, both the big and the small—even the stupid Christmas tree. Charlie deserves the chance to rise to the occasion and meet those needs. Although there was a time, before our separation, when he might not have listened to my needs, he has demonstrated now that he is ready, willing, and able to do it. It's unfair to treat him like an old version of himself. It's unfair to myself to stay silent about my needs just because the old Charlie wasn't listening.

It makes me uncomfortable to talk about what I need and want. Like so many of us, I grew up learning how to make myself small. That training took a lot of forms: "God first, others second, and self last." "Selflessness is its own reward." "Love is when the other person's happiness is more important than your own." I had parents who pushed me to be fierce and independent, but even they were no match for the world's domestication, its constant pressure for good little girls to grow up into selfless little women. We are told that selflessness is in our nature. As the great Mahatma Gandhi once put it, "Man can never be a woman's equal in the spirit of selfless service with which nature has endowed her."

I had parents who pushed me to be fierce and independent, but even they were no match for the world's domestication, its constant pressure for good little girls to grow up into selfless little women.

In these subtle, not so subtle, direct,

and indirect ways, we are raised to understand that women are born to be selfless and that, impossibly, men are not. If selflessness is supposedly in our nature, then what does it mean when we don't feel selfless? What does it say about us as "good women" when we want our partners to take care of *our* needs?

These are the ideas that shame us into silence. Being unhappy, dissatisfied, and unfulfilled somehow feels better than being *selfish,* so we choose to say nothing. And this is the sad truth of why we engage in passive immobility, why we are so desperate for our spouses to be mind readers. We want them to know our needs because speaking them for ourselves triggers shame.

This is one of the areas in which I've had to do some of the most substantial work on my truth trench. I've had to dig out the lies that got planted there by a world committed to making women small and then plant in their place these fundamental truths:

- It is fair and reasonable for me to want my needs met and to communicate them.
- It is unfair and unreasonable for me to expect my husband to read my mind.
- There is nothing wrong with me for wanting my husband's help.
- It is not my job to be selfless.

These truths have been hard to internalize, but I'm getting there with practice. I have begun the difficult work of speaking my needs to Charlie, even when it feels uncomfortable. I've learned to ask him to take down the tree for me instead of putting on a dramatic display of pretend incompetence to get him to do it. And what do you know? We're getting along *so much* better these days as a result. (I'd also like to add that it doesn't feel great to admit these things about myself, but I'm willing to bet, dear reader, you've been in my shoes, too.)

Self-care begins with expressing my needs. Sharing them communicates to others how I want to be supported, reminding them and myself that I am worthy of being valued and respected. It's a frightening process, this determination to just say what the hell I need. I could write an entire book on why I think that is. It could be the apprehension of being called selfish, demanding, or entitled (words that often tend to be reserved for women who choose to speak up). It could be the memory of asking for things and having them belittled or ignored. Or perhaps it is the deep-seated fear that people don't think I'm worth the effort it would take to meet those needs, that maybe my habit of keeping my needs to myself has trained people to believe that I don't require much effort and that having me around wouldn't be worth it if they actually had to do something, if it had to be a two-way street.

Of course, none of that is true, but self-care must include the difficult work of finally releasing these misconceptions about ourselves.

I am worthy of having my needs met. I deserve two-way streets. And the people who love me would be more than happy to give these things to me, if only I would say what I need.

Self-care is not expecting people to read my mind.

Self-care is being brave and vulnerable enough to tell people what I need—to do the thing that came so easily to me as a child but that domestication has trained out of me.

Self-care is telling my husband that I want him to take down the Christmas tree.

It's as simple and as complicated as that.

Cultivate Your Truth Trench

- **Even the people who know you best can't read your mind.** It feels good when people know you so intimately they can predict your needs without your having to say a word, but no one can do that perfectly or at all times. Expressing your needs is an act of self-care. It's okay to advocate for yourself and communicate your desires openly and honestly.
- **Mind reading brings anxiety; open communication brings connection.** Practice being brave and vulnerable by sharing your needs with your partner. Speaking honestly about your needs allows your partner to rise to the occasion, showing you that you are loved and that your needs are important.
- **Self-care in relationships is neither selfless nor selfish.** You will never feel loved and fulfilled in your romantic partnership if you constantly prioritize your partner's needs over your own. You do not have to be selfless to be loved, and it isn't selfish to tell your partner what you need.
- **You deserve two-way streets.** Advocating for yourself is an essential aspect of sensible self-care. Take ownership of your well-being by expressing your needs and boundaries confidently. Don't settle for one-way streets that don't take your needs into account.

Chapter Five

Car Filth

Nothing tells me that my husband has a death wish more than when he mentions how dirty my car is. I will hold my tongue in the name of peace about a lot of things, but not this. Those are fightin' words.

I am the default parent. Because I am the one doing most of the parenting on weekdays, I also happen to be the family chauffeur, and I do *a lot* of driving. We are really fortunate that my son Roman's elementary school is only two miles from our home. Unfortunately, because of our late-summer move to a new school district, the only preschool that had availability for my daughter was thirty minutes away from our apartment. So, between drop-offs and pickups, I spend about two hours a day in the car just for her.

Then there are all the trips to school events, sports practice, playgrounds, the grocery store. Oh, and let's not forget the forty-five minutes or more I spend every day in car line at *two different schools.* My car has become my office, my powder room, and sometimes my nap room (those car lines are brutal; I keep a pillow in the passenger seat). Point is, I'm doing a whole lot of living in that car.

I'll get to the back seat in a minute, but first let me explain about the front half of my car. It's filthy, alright? I'm not going to pretend it's not. Charlie tries not to give me too much grief about the back where the kids sit, but he is mystified as to why the front, where presumably only I sit, is such a disaster.

But the front seat is where I'm doing life! On any given day I have my purse, a backpack with my tech, and a few books in tow so that I can work from any place with coffee and good Wi-Fi. I usually have my makeup case with me so that at red lights I can crookedly apply my eyeliner in the rearview mirror. I buy more Starbucks skinny vanilla lattes in a day than I have cup holders in my car. As if I don't make enough mess on my own, I also have all the crap that my kids hand me from the back seat that I'm supposed to find something to do with.

So, yeah, my front seat is a catastrophe.

The back seat . . . I don't know if I even have the energy to talk about it. Lost french fries from Happy Meals are smashed into the floorboards. Dark rings have pooled on every fabric surface where drinks were spilled and never properly cleaned. And don't even get me started on the car seats.

It doesn't help matters that every time we head to the car, the kids have handfuls of toys they simply can't leave the house without. Of course, by the time we get back home they have lost all strength in their arms and can't *possibly* be asked to carry their stuff back in. My hands are filled with as much of my own crap as I can manage, so in the car their stuff stays.

Like most spouses who aren't the default parent and don't understand any of this, my husband sometimes likes to *helpfully* point out that there are things I could do to avoid the mess.

"Don't let them eat in the car and there won't be food mess," he tells me. "Don't let them take toys to the car and they won't accumulate in there."

The thing is, I actually do all those things. For every one time my kids get a Happy Meal in the car, there are at least ten other times I make them wait until we get home. Every toy left behind in the car was once made to be brought back inside, only for another toy to take its place the next day. I do have rules for my car. I just don't always have the mental energy for the fight. There's really no other way to say it. The ones who get it, get it. The ones who don't, probably aren't the default parent. Some days, I just don't feel like arguing with my kids. Other days, I'm weighing out the cost-to-benefit ratio between the mental labor of arguing and the physical labor of cleaning up whatever mess gets made. The mess almost always comes out looking like the better option.

Besides, neither I nor the kids seem to be too bothered by the mess.

The mess bothers Charlie, though. He wants me to have a clean car, one that I can be proud of. To him, the solution is so simple. Lay down some ground rules. Enforce them strictly. Don't budge. But he doesn't understand what it's like to have tiny, constantly ravenous and stimulation-seeking children in the back seat. He hasn't felt the drain it puts on your spirit to have to keep saying no to your children, hasn't had to make the choice between cleanliness and sanity.

I don't fault him for not understanding. I just don't want to be chided about the car's condition or given a well-meaning but unhelpful lecture about how to keep it clean. After having one too many disagreements over this issue, I finally communicated this to him. High five for no more mind reading!

I was proud of how we handled the conversation. We showed up as a team, us against the problem instead of us against each other. Since a big part of self-care is clearly and kindly saying what we need and allowing the people we love to rise to meet us there, I told Charlie exactly what I needed, and he listened.

I explained that the mess, the debris, the chaos—they don't really bother me. My car is a rolling command center. It works just fine for me, messy or not. Since the mess doesn't bother me, I choose to be flexible with my car rules. Bending the rules for my kids every now and then is less of a drain on me than arguing with them for the sake of a clean car.

When I saw that Charlie was tracking with me, I next shared with him how his consternation about the mess was what actually caused me stress. I told him that it makes me feel like he doesn't understand my life when he boils the car mess down to something so black-and-white. It's not as simple as enforcing a few rules, and the reason he doesn't understand that is because *he has never had to do what I do.* I don't need suggestions for how to keep it clean. I would rather he just understand that I've made the choice for peace over cleanliness and support me in that.

I don't need suggestions for how to keep it clean. I would rather he just understand that I've made the choice for peace over cleanliness and support me in that.

Communicating these feelings to him felt so good. He listened, absorbing everything. After a few moments he made me an offer. He explained that he hates seeing me in a filthy car because it makes him feel like he's failing me as a husband. The state of my car says something about how well he's taking care of me, he said. The filthy car feels like evidence of his inadequacy. So, instead of staying after me to keep it clean, he decided to make it his job to clean my car. *Ahh, the gift of a husband who has gone to therapy.*

We agreed, and his weekend car cleanings are just a part of our routine now.

Sometimes, self-care is about drawing limits and setting boundaries. Charlie had an issue with my car being dirty and accidentally made it *my* issue. Too often we take ownership of other people's expectations of us, deciding to hold ourselves accountable to their expectations instead of our own. Unfortunately, that path will never lead to fulfillment. Remember, *we will never get full eating self-care potato chips.* Swallowing down handfuls of someone else's expectations in the name of "taking care of ourselves" will only lead to emptiness. Probably some indigestion, too.

The delicate truth of self-care is that sometimes the things we need to do to take care of ourselves are hard to swallow. We have to set boundaries and stand our ground. We have to live by our own rules, casting off the expectations of others when they don't serve us. We have to protect our peace and stand up for our needs, even when no one understands. That work is hard but always worth it.

The delicate truth of self-care is that sometimes the things we need to do to take care of ourselves are hard to swallow. We have to set boundaries and stand our ground. We have to live by our own rules, casting off the expectations of others when they don't serve us. We have to protect our peace and stand up for our needs, even when no one understands. That work is hard but always worth it.

This is how self-care shows up in the difficult conversations with our partners. You should be able to tell your partner what you need, as well as what you don't need, and to feel heard—not just to feel heard, but to actually *be* heard. If you don't feel safe to communicate even the most trivial of your needs to your partner, or if you can communicate your needs but see no action as a result, it's time to take a hard look at your relationship.

Where is the communication breaking down? Is it happening because you aren't sharing your needs? Or is it because your partner isn't hearing them? What is the reason for the lack of communication or effort? Where is the impasse?

Love yourself enough to ask these hard questions. Dig into them, for the sake of your peace and your partner's. The answers to these questions matter. *You matter*. The entire point of self-care is to reinforce to yourself and to others that *all your needs, even the ones that don't make sense to other people matter!*

The answers to these questions matter. *You matter.* The entire point of self-care is to reinforce to yourself and to others that *all your needs, even the ones that don't make sense to other people matter!*

A whole freaking lot.

Even when your car is filthy; maybe especially then.

Cultivate Your Truth Trench

- **Self-care is living by your own expectations.** With the best intentions, other people will push their expectations onto you. But they are not living your life; they do not know your circumstances. Determine to live according to your own expectations and set healthy boundaries if your partner (or anyone, for that matter) tries to make you internalize their expectations of you.
- **It is possible for someone to care for you the wrong way.** You deserve to be cared for the way that makes you feel loved. It is good for your self-esteem and your relationship to tell your partner, clearly and specifically, that the way they show up for you doesn't make you feel loved or cared for. Then, tell them the right way to do it.
- **Prioritize your authentic needs, even if they don't make sense to others.** You are allowed to prioritize your peace of mind over what anyone else says is appropriate or correct. There is no "right" way to do things—only what is right for you.
- **Self-care means having difficult but honest conversations.** It is not loving to yourself or to others to bottle up your feelings and needs. Honesty, vulnerability, and a commitment to having the hard conversations lead to a better self-image and better relationships.

Chapter Six

Dinner After Dark

Nourishment comes in many forms. As a child, nothing filled me like the simple moments at the kitchen table. It was a place where dreams were hatched and stories told with my parents at my side. Every evening, we came together to share stories about the events of our day, from the magical to the mundane. It was a special time for me, as an only child, to connect with my parents. It was also a wonderful opportunity to watch them connect with each other—creating intimacy together in a way that warmed my heart and, paradoxically, grossed me out.

Naturally, I have always looked forward to creating those special memories with my own kids. It was impressed upon me that establishing this kind of dinner dynamic starts early. It begins with teaching mealtime routines and table manners, and eventually involves modeling wholesome and engaging conversation. I know it can be done. My parents have home videos of me at four years old, sitting maturely at the dinner table with my palms pressed together in prayer, reciting the *daily bread* blessing with faltering but adorable ease. I wanted that for my kids. I wanted it for me and Charlie, too. What better way to show our children how much we love each other, how safe and secure their parents' relationship is, than to demonstrate it for them every day at the dinner table?

With that as the standard, I started table-training my kids the moment they were able to sit up on their own. I tried to have dinner ready around the same time every night, for the sake of routine. I cooked regularly, always trying exciting new recipes that I hoped would dazzle. I was so excited the first time I got to push my son's highchair up to the table and dip small helpings from our plates onto his little tray. Charlie and I laughed as he smeared sweet potatoes between his fingers and clumsily raised them to his mouth. It felt like I was already on my way to making dinnertime magic.

Things got a bit more complicated when, a few months before my son's second birthday, my daughter came along. It's tough to have a family dinner when there is a toddler at the table and a newborn at the breast. Babies don't care much about your routines, and my daughter was no exception. Although mealtimes had been relatively simple when it was just the three of us, adding one more to the equation threw things out of balance. It was a beautiful time, watching us grow to a family of four, but it was also a lot more chaos than I had anticipated. Gradually, I had to let go of bits of my dinnertime routine. Home-cooked meals were replaced by DiGiorno pizza and Door Dashed Chinese food. Instead of gathering around the table, we took our meals wherever we happened to be stationed when the food was ready. Usually, that meant me on the couch, nursing my daughter with a paper carton of fried rice by my side, and my husband eating his food over the sink. So much for the portrait of marital togetherness and familial bliss we wanted to model for the kids.

You do what you have to do in the early years. We were doing the best we could, and we still made plenty of memories. I figured that in a few years, when the kids were both a bit more independent, I'd get back to re-creating the dinnertime magic from my childhood. Charlie and I would look on with pride as the kids regaled us with the events of their day; they would feign disgust at us casually flirting over our dinner plates, pretending our public displays of affection were "cringe." It was just a matter of patience.

When the kids were finally both in preschool, I began trying to resume my dinner routine. By then, I had learned about the supposed importance of everyone eating the same meal at dinnertime. No substitutions, no made-to-order meal requests. One dinner is made, and everyone will like it. No exceptions. That's what the gurus said, anyway.

I tried this with all the best intentions. I tried *a lot* of things with the best intentions. But it still just didn't seem like family dinners gelled the way they had when I was a kid. Everything just sort of felt like chaos. Delightful chaos, but chaos nonetheless.

Striving to keep up with this image of what dinnertime should look like was beginning to take a toll on my relationship with Charlie. I was often flustered and irritable by the time dinner was served. My attempts at mealtime conversation with Charlie, to share and reconnect, were drowned out by the crash of upturned sippy cups and fistfuls of food splatting to the floor. And instead of embracing the chaos as a necessary step in our journey, I fiercely resisted it.

Insisting our family dinners conform with this vision of mine, despite the obvious incompatibility, was making me miserable. I snapped at Charlie for no reason. Conversations turned cold. The dinner table shifted from a sanctuary of love and harmony to a battleground we had to march through. We were just trying to survive.

Eventually, we gave up trying altogether.

Ideals are lovely, useful things. They give us something to aspire to, something to work toward. But sometimes ideals don't align with reality. Life is often chaotic with shifting dynamics and a lot of moving parts. Sometimes, we just need to do what makes sense. Charlie and I realized that we highly valued dinnertime together—the opportunity to share good food over glasses of wine and to reconnect after a long day. That was just something we were not willing to sacrifice anymore. We also wanted to enjoy dinnertime with our kids. It was important to begin establishing the routine for family dinners even if we couldn't have the kind of connection and conversations that we wanted just yet. The only way to have both, we realized, was to have two dinners.

Ideals are lovely, useful things. They give us something to aspire to, something to work toward. But sometimes ideals don't align with reality. Life is often chaotic with shifting dynamics and a lot of moving parts. Sometimes, we just need to do what makes sense.

Self-care sometimes means doing something unconventional. It means forgetting *should* and focusing on *can* and asking yourself not what *should* I do, but what *can* I do?

Self-care sometimes means doing something unconventional. It means forgetting *should* and focusing on *can* and asking yourself not what *should* I do, but what *can* I do?

Expectations tell us what we *should* do. We get so fixated on meeting the expectation that we never stop to ask if all that effort is actually making us happy, if it's actually what we want.

Creativity shows us what we *can* do. It allows us to come up with solutions that defy our expectations and make us happier and more fulfilled. Expectations starve; creativity nourishes.

So, Charlie and I got creative. We decided that in order to give the kids the mealtime routine they deserved, without sacrificing our meals together as a couple, we would have two separate meals. It seemed like a lot of work at first, but it's actually worked out quite well for us.

In the evenings, around 5:00 PM, Charlie and I can both be found in the kitchen. He begins working on preparing the exquisite cuisine of elementary schoolers—chicken nuggets, hot dogs, macaroni and cheese. The kids get to request what they want, and since these dishes are easy to prepare, Charlie has no problem making two separate dinners for them. Sometimes the kids ask to order pizza or sushi (yes, my four- and six-year-old love it, which is something that still surprises me), and Charlie will occasionally indulge them.

While he prepares their meals, I start working on our grown-up dinner. I've come to really enjoy bustling about in the kitchen, basting chicken and chopping vegetables with Charlie nearby. The kids usually come sit at the kitchen island while we cook. Sometimes, they bring their tablets and ask us to watch funny YouTube clips with them, other times they whip up an art project with Play-Doh or markers and we look on with pride. It's become one of my favorite parts of our day because we're just so *together*. It looks nothing like the dinners from my childhood, and yet it's perfect.

It looks nothing like the dinners from my childhood, and yet it's perfect.

The kids are usually finishing up their dinner around the time that my and Charlie's meal is coming out of the oven. I offer them a sample of what I've cooked, which often is promptly spat out. We have, however, had occasional triumphs and discovered a new food that the kids enjoy. It's my way of expanding their palates without forcing them to eat meals that their taste buds just aren't quite ready for. They tend to be agreeable about trying these new things because they know it's okay if they don't like it. We make progress without the fight.

Charlie starts the kids' bedtime routine while I put the final touches on our meal. When the kids are all settled, we give them their good-night kisses and head back to the kitchen for our own dinner. Sometimes it's a romantic dinner table with candles lit and our French doors open to let the night air in. Other times, it's exhausted heads drooped lazily over paper plates at the kitchen island. It's not the atmosphere that matters but the connection. A priceless moment when conversation knows no bounds—uninterrupted by the needs of our little ones.

This is how we nourish ourselves.

It took me a long time to accept that self-care meant discarding my idea of what *should* be and opening up to the expansive opportunity of what *can* be. I'm done being tethered to expectations of myself that no longer serve me. I'm not building my life around what anyone else says should make sense. No longer bound by limiting beliefs and external expectations, my life is now being shaped with intentionality—based on what will bring fulfillment and joy. That is true self-care.

It took me a long time to accept that self-care meant discarding my idea of what *should* be and opening up to the expansive opportunity of what *can* be.

Too often, we settle for potato chips because that's what our parents ate. We build our lives around the traditions we learned from them. Those of us who were fortunate to have happy childhoods tend to romanticize them, holding up the lives our parents created for us as the gold standard—the absolute ideal. To our dismay, we discover that the things that nourished our parents, like family dinner at the table, only leave us with that empty-calorie, ate-a-whole-bag-of-chips-and-still-feel-hungry feeling. We hold our bellies in pain, wondering why the traditions that filled our parents leave us feeling so desperately empty.

Nourishing self-care means creating our own traditions. Forging our own paths. It means choosing to be unconventional, to do what works for us instead of what worked for our parents, our neighbors, or our friends. It means not taking the parenting gurus too seriously, to understand that even the best and most well-meaning advice might not work for our own family. And, to that end, it means letting go of shame when we make choices that are different from what those people say is "the right way."

When we decide to boldly pursue the things that truly fill us up, we find the world opening to us in ways we never thought it could. And yes, even something as simple as having two dinners instead of one can be a transformative act of self-care.

When we decide to boldly pursue the things that truly fill us up, we find the world opening to us in ways we never thought it could.

Charlie and I are better parents, better partners, and better people when we take this small bit of time for ourselves each evening. Self-care, at least at this stage of our lives, is forsaking *should* and embracing the breathtaking magic of *can* instead.

Cultivate Your Truth Trench

- **Embrace creativity over convention.** Instead of clinging to rigid expectations of what your life should look like, embrace creativity and flexibility. Focus on what you can do rather than what you should do. Allow yourself the freedom to make choices that work for your unique family dynamic.
- **Find surrender in the seasons.** It's easy to tell ourselves that certain things will last forever, but most things in life only last for a season. Sometimes, self-care simply means allowing life to accommodate the needs of the season. Joy and ease can come from surrendering to what life calls for at the time, without letting go of your vision for the future.
- **Nourish new traditions.** Some traditions from your childhood might not work for your blossoming family. You can honor and appreciate your parents' traditions while embracing with openness the possibility for new traditions—ones that reflect the needs and composition of your own family.
- **Self-care is personal.** Understand that self-care is a deeply personal journey. It's about tuning in to your own needs, desires, and values and making choices that align with them. Let go of shame or guilt associated with doing things your own way.

Chapter Seven

Ports of Call

It all started when we arrived at the port and the cruise ship was not there.

I had spent weeks planning a special cruise vacation for my family. Charlie and I had moved back in together only a few short months prior, and I wanted to give us and the children a little getaway, something to help put the separation behind us and to begin settling into our new, reconciled normal. I envisioned this trip as a gift from me to my family. Charlie was preoccupied with getting his new business off the ground and had a lot of stress on his plate, so I decided to handle all the planning myself. It felt good to take care of everything. I'm not a naturally organized person, and attention to detail is not my strong suit. I was proud of myself for stepping out of my comfort zone and accomplishing something that's hard for me.

The night before the trip, Charlie was getting some pre-vacation anxiety. He flitted around the apartment, looking lost. "Did you pack the sunscreen? What about the kids' floaties? Should we have picked up some motion sickness pills just in case?"

I assured him that he didn't have to worry about a thing—I had taken care of every detail. I saw Charlie try to relax and enjoy being taken care of, but he does know me better than anyone in the world. It was hard for him to not feel at least a little skeptical of my ability to take care of everything without missing at least one important detail.

It was an eight-hour drive to the port, and our boarding time was 11:30 AM. We woke the kids in the middle of the night, still in their jammies, and slipped them out to the car. Charlie and I were exhausted but enjoyed getting to stay up all night chatting and sipping gas station coffee while the children slumbered.

Soon, the sun was up, and we arrived at our destination. Having sailed out of this port before, I knew that the ship was obscured just behind the enormous walls of the parking deck. We made our way around back to give the kids their first look at the ship.

They squealed with glee as I rolled the windows down for them to get a better look. I drew in a sharp breath of anticipation as we rounded the corner, then let it out heavily in dismay.

There was no ship there.

A sinking feeling made its way into my stomach. There was absolutely no way the ship wouldn't have arrived by now. I was suddenly aware of just how empty the parking structure was, how utterly desolate the whole port looked.

I usually miss small details, not ship-sized ones. There had to be an explanation that didn't involve me royally screwing up. Horrified, I began to wonder if I had gotten the dates wrong. I yanked my phone off the charger and checked the dates on our sailing confirmation. I had the dates right, thankfully. But then, I noticed a detail I hadn't seen before.

Three Day Cruise—Departing from Port Canaveral, Florida.

And we were idling slack-jawed in a parking structure in New Orleans, Louisiana.

Somehow, in all my attention to the tiniest of details, I had overlooked the most important one—where to find the ship.

First, I began to tremble, then I began to sob. Not knowing what else to do, or how to make the situation better, I turned numbly to the back seat and explained to my precious, wide-eyed children that I had made a mistake. It would be impossible to get to Florida before the ship departed, and there were no flights that would get us there in time either. Our vacation was ruined.

While the children wailed and Charlie stared vacantly at the spot where the ship should have been, I sat, dumbfounded, in the front seat. I felt paralyzed. In my efforts to give the perfect gift to my family, I had made the *one* mistake that couldn't be smoothed over or worked around. It was over.

A past version of myself, the one from before our separation and my hard work in therapy, would have quickly made a bad situation worse by getting defensive. I might have found reasons to lash out at everyone else because exploding is sometimes the only way for unhealed people to cope with shame. I wouldn't have been able to accept that I'd made a mistake and ask for help fixing it because I needed to be perfect. If I wasn't perfect, then I wasn't good. And if I wasn't good, then why would I expect anyone to help me out of my self-created mess?

I wouldn't have been able to accept that I'd made a mistake and ask for help fixing it because I needed to be perfect. If I wasn't perfect, then I wasn't good. And if I wasn't good, then why would I expect anyone to help me out of my self-created mess?

But I had been doing the meticulous work of self-care, learning that I can make a mistake and still be a good person. I am allowed to screw up, and I am allowed to feel my feelings about that. I can let other people help me out of sticky situations, even the ones I created all by myself, because people love me, and I am worthy of receiving their help.

So, rather than sulking and suffering alone, or misdirecting my disappointment in myself at my innocent family, I asked Charlie to help me make a new plan. It took some time. We had to make a lot of phone calls, have a lot of ideas shot down as impossible, then form a new idea and try again. All this while trying to keep two very unhappy kids calm in the back seat. But thankfully, mercifully, we made it happen. I convinced the cruise line to give us a refund in the form of a credit toward a future cruise, and Charlie worked with a Disney World cast member to get us a one-day pass to the Magic Kingdom and a one-night stay at one of their budget-friendly resort hotels. It would be modest, much less extravagant than our cruise would have been, but it was something.

We were exhausted and still an eight-hour drive away from our new destination, which, admittedly, wasn't great. But we were going to do, together, whatever it took to salvage this family getaway I'd worked so hard to create. And we did. We were going to make it happen after all.

It was then that I finally dissolved into a puddle of grateful, comforted tears. There was no magic in all of Disney that would outmagic that moment—the magic of loving myself enough to ask for help—and the nourishing self-care of fixing the problem instead of wallowing in it.

There is a psychologist named John Gottman who developed a pretty useful model for helping couples manage sticky situations like my cruise disaster. His model distinguishes between *solvable* problems and *persistent* problems. His research has found that nearly 70 percent of all marital conflict is made up of persistent problems—that is, problems that stem from fundamental differences in couples' personalities, values, or lifestyle needs. They are problems that a couple will come back to again and again. Solvable problems, on the other hand, are situational. The conflict is temporary, and a solution can be found if the couple chooses to work together as a team. He suggests that, in order to be happiest as individuals and as a couple, both partners need to work together to resolve the solvable problems as they arise. That way, they will have the time and energy to return to the persistent problems that will take much more work.

Self-care, in that moment in the car, was choosing to solve a solvable problem together with my husband instead of letting the problem fester. No doubt, if we had thrown our hands in the air and returned home with our time and money wasted, what could have been a solvable problem would have become a persistent problem. Frustration and resentment would have built up between us. It would have come up in arguments down the road, perhaps with Charlie reminding me of how careless and irresponsible I can be, how I am always failing to think things through. I would have believed those words because they matched what I already believed about myself. But while I might have internalized those words silently, I probably would have exploded outwardly. I would have acted wounded, angry. Would have thrown his own mistakes back in his face, and round-and-round we'd go.

Self-care, in that moment in the car, was choosing to solve a solvable problem together with my husband instead of letting the problem fester.

So instead, I chose to sit in the discomfort of asking Charlie to help me solve the problem. Self-care looked like Charlie and I making phone calls that were, honestly, *so* embarrassing. Admitting to complete strangers what a stupid mistake I had made and asking for their charity in helping me fix it was kind of a new low. But self-care was being okay with feeling embarrassed because I recognized that screwing up is human, normal, common. Self-care was also thinking about my future self, the one who would either look back on this with shame at my mistake or with pride for how I fixed it. I wanted my future self to have pride in me.

I'd made a mistake, but I was still worthy. I'd made a mistake, but I was capable of fixing it. I proved that I could fix it—that *we* could fix it, together. And now, when we look back on that moment, we can laugh. I get to feel proud of myself for solving the problem, for working with my husband to make a bad thing good again. My self-esteem and self-efficacy get to grow, not shrink.

I think some people get the idea that self-care is this really *woo-woo* philosophy. *Be mellow. Take baths. Don't let things get under your skin.* They don't realize that self-care can be practical, methodical, and evidence based. Toxic self-care culture would have told me that fixing this disaster was as simple as driving back home and washing the shame away with a hot bath and a glass of wine. Maybe doing a little retail therapy on Amazon while I soaked. But real self-care, the kind that nourishes, is so much deeper than that. It's about going to therapy, doing the uncomfortable but necessary work of growth, and implementing what we've learned in the hard moments in life. It's about solving problems instead of

I think some people get the idea that self-care is this really *woo-woo* philosophy. *Be mellow. Take baths. Don't let things get under your skin.* They don't realize that self-care can be practical, methodical, and evidence based.

medicating them with the useless Band-Aids of bubble baths and consumerism.

You'll arrive at many wrong ports throughout your lifetime. You'll make the wrong career move. You'll make parenting mistakes. You'll hurt someone you care about. True self-care is being brave enough to admit you messed up. It is being gracious enough to forgive yourself. It is being audacious enough to ask for help instead of fumbling to fix it on your own.

You'll arrive at many wrong ports throughout your lifetime. You'll make the wrong career move. You'll make parenting mistakes. You'll hurt someone you care about. True self-care is being brave enough to admit you messed up. It is being gracious enough to forgive yourself. It is being audacious enough to ask for help instead of fumbling to fix it on your own.

As for me and my family's spoiled cruise? In an interesting turn of events, I've decided to use part of the advance for this book to schedule a new cruise for me and my family. I'm thinking of it as a corrective experience, a do-over, if you will. There's something beautiful about telling this story right now, understanding that *this story in particular* helped me secure a book deal. That being vulnerable, willing to laugh at myself and able to share a humiliating story to teach about the importance of self-care that *actually fulfills*, has given me the opportunity to try again.

This time, I'm letting my husband help me from the start—not because I'm dumb or can't be trusted to do it right but because *I have a partner*, and I deserve to not have to do it alone.

Self-care, this time around, will mean not loading up an unnecessary burden on my shoulders. It'll mean accepting help because I am worthy of it. It'll mean letting my husband participate in the planning because he loves me and wants us to succeed.

And, dear reader, it'll also mean triple-checking that port of departure before we leave.

Cultivate Your Truth Trench

- **Sometimes, you have to face the shame.** Instead of succumbing to shame or defensiveness when faced with your mistakes, embrace vulnerability and growth. Recognize that making mistakes is a part of being human, and allow yourself the grace to learn and grow from them.
- **It is a gift to let others help you.** Practice self-care by seeking support and collaboration from loved ones when facing challenges. Asking for help is not a sign of weakness but a courageous act of self-care that can lead to creative solutions and strengthened relationships.
- **Solve the solvable problems; live to "fight" another day.** Prioritize resolving solvable problems together as a team to prevent them from escalating into persistent issues that can strain the relationship. Self-care in relationships often means tackling the small problems quickly so you have the strength and resolve to handle the big problems later.
- **Quick self-care fixes seldom do the trick.** Self-care goes beyond superficial "easy" fixes and encompasses practical, methodical, and evidence-based approaches to problem-solving and personal growth. It involves confronting discomfort, seeking therapy, and implementing the things you've learned when life gets hard.

Chapter Eight

The Honey-Do List

Sometimes, it feels like all I do is make lists: to-do lists, to-buy lists, to-organize-later lists, lists of things the kids need for school, lists of obligations I committed to but definitely don't have time for, lists of things I will say to that asshole ex-boss of mine if I we ever cross paths again. If it exists in the world (or in my imagination), I've probably made a list about it.

Lists are useful things. They help me stay organized, less distractible. When there are lists, things feel ordered. Structured. Manageable. But lists can also feel overwhelming—a reminder of all the things I have left to do. As a person who is already prone to anxiety, I can become easily stressed and defeated when my lists are too many or too long.

I have a husband, someone with whom I share all the household responsibilities. When we got married, I assumed we would share those responsibilities equally, or at least equitably. We both have jobs. We both have functioning eyeballs. We both can look around the house when we have a moment to spare and see what needs to be done. Taking care of a household, then, should be a matter of both of us seeing what needs to be done and doing it or, if it can't be done right then, adding it to our lists for later.

But that wasn't my experience, at least not for the first many years of my marriage. As we got into the groove of our daily shared routines, I noticed that my lists were filling up—page after page of things to remember, chores to complete, schedules to manage—yet Charlie seemed to have no lists, at least not ones pertaining to the house and the kids. When I pointed out that my to-do lists were getting out of control, he countered with "Just tell me what you need help with, and I'll do it." I hated the idea that *our mess, our responsibilities*, and *our kids* were things that I needed to ask for help with since they were *ours*, but I asked anyway. And inevitably, things still didn't get done.

He forgot.

He got too busy.

He'd get to it when he had time.

And why did I insist on things being done on my timeline, anyway?

This was a persistent problem in our marriage, one that we are only just beginning to understand and address. For years, I complained about his lack of participation around the house, and he countered by reminding me that he would help with anything as long as I asked.

At this, I would balk every time. I had worked hard to stop my passive immobility—to tell him what I needed instead of expecting him to read my mind. But the thing was, I didn't really see domestic partnership as something that needed to be asked for. It required a pair of eyeballs and a sense of duty. You don't have to be a mind reader to know that the clean dishes need to be taken out of the dishwasher or that the dried toothpaste needs to be scraped off the bathroom countertop. Why did I have to ask? Perhaps more importantly, why did I bother asking when things went undone anyway?

When I addressed this with Charlie, he apologized. He said that he has a hard time remembering and keeping track of tasks like that, which I understood. He has ADHD. It significantly impairs his executive functioning—his ability to make plans, focus on goals, and juggle tasks successfully. He said that in order for me to "help him help me" (his words, not mine), it would be better if I would make a honey-do list for him. Write it all down and stick it on the refrigerator so that he can't miss it.

One more list for me to make. One more thing for *me* to keep track of if I wanted his participation in *our* responsibilities. One more thing for me to oversee. I wanted to be understanding, especially since he can't help that his ADHD likes to Riverdance all over his executive functioning. But I just couldn't help feeling like the real problem was that he simply didn't see all the tasks of keeping house as a priority. At least, not *his* priority. It was my priority. And if I needed "help" with that, then it was up to me to manage and delegate accordingly. In other words, to make him a list.

This list making and task-tracking and overseeing of household tasks has a name. It's called *mental load*. Mental load is the invisible work of organizing, delegating, managing, and remembering the things that have to be done. It's more than the task itself, such as getting the kids ready for school. It's the labor of checking the school calendar to see if they need to take anything special that day, reviewing homework, remembering what foods can and cannot be brought to the classroom, and packing equipment for after-school activities. Every task has a

This list making and task-tracking and overseeing of household tasks has a name. It's called *mental load.* Mental load is the invisible work of organizing, delegating, managing, and remembering the things that have to be done.

list of subtasks, all of which have to be remembered and executed, most of which go unnoticed and unappreciated. And even in many progressive homes, the majority of this invisible labor still falls on women's shoulders.

I had become better at delegating some of this mental load to my husband, but I found myself being let down again and again. He would forget to take care of the thing I asked him to do, and because I had mentally checked it off my to-do list when I delegated it to him, I didn't catch that the thing hadn't been done until the last possible second. I was left scrambling to take care of something at the eleventh hour and usually taking the blame (from the kids, or the teachers, or the coaches) for doing a bad job of it. I had kept track of what needed to be done by making my own list of responsibilities and had, from that list, entrusted a few important tasks to my husband. And he forgot.

Why couldn't he make his own damn list? How was it fair that in a house with two capable adults, one of us had to manage all the tasks—not just the execution but also the planning and management of those tasks—while the other got to passively receive tasks? Why didn't he think he needed to be responsible for managing his own to-do list?

In her book *Fair Play*, Eve Rodsky explains why this inequitable distribution of household labor falls unfairly on women instead of men. Sadly, it boils down to how society tends to view men's time versus women's. Men's time is often viewed as finite, a valuable resource not to be squandered. Women's time, on the other hand, is like sand: It's in such abundance that it can't even be measured. There is some scientific evidence that even *we women* hold these disparate views of our time's value compared to men's. It's an idea that was spoon-fed to us by a society that prioritizes men's time over our own that many of us have accidentally internalized. It's not our fault, and to be fair, it's not our husbands' fault either. It's how we all were trained. The only way to fix this imbalance, according to Rodsky, is for both men and women, husbands and wives, to consider each other's time and contributions equitably.

I spend a lot of time online challenging men who don't believe men and women should show up as equals in their marriages. An argument that a staggering number of men have made in these conversations is that men are basically toddlers. If we want healthy and happy marriages, we should treat our husbands as such. That means we should assume that they are emotionally unintelligent and unable to communicate their thoughts and feelings to us in a constructive way. It also means giving them positive reinforcement when they behave the way we want them to, reassuring them with constant praise, and yes, making goddamn honey-do lists for them. When I ask these men whether it feels shameful to infantilize themselves this way, they matter-of-factly say, "Of course not; this is just how we're made."

It's a shame that our culture has taught these men to think such things about themselves.

My husband is not a toddler. He is a grown man. I am not more emotionally intelligent than him. My time is not less valuable than his. I do not have more of it. I am not better suited for the invisible administrative labor that a home requires. And it's certainly not my job to be his mother. Our time is equal, both in its quantity and in its value. It is our job, together, to figure out who owns which tasks and to take full responsibility for the tasks we own. That means owning not just the execution of those tasks but also the delegation, management, and oversight of them. I will not patronize my husband by treating him like he's one of my children instead of the grown and capable man I married. We must work together as equitable partners.

Note my use of the term *equitable* rather than *equal.* In my household, the labor really can't be divided *equally* between me and Charlie. He works more than I do and brings in the majority of our household income. Often, he works well into the night with very little rest. He has deadlines and deliverables that cannot be rescheduled and people counting on him to get his job done so that they can do theirs. My job, on the other hand, is flexible. I am self-employed, so I can move my schedule around as needed. The only pressure I have is the kind I put on myself, and I try my best to be a fair boss in that regard.

I do not expect Charlie to share the household tasks *equally*. That burden would be too much for him, and even though it would technically be "equal" it would also be unfair. So, we divide the household labor *equitably*. This means that we consider each other's work schedules, skill sets, and personal responsibilities to ensure that the division of labor is fair and balanced, even if it doesn't result in an exact 50/50 split of tasks. In this way, we acknowledge and accommodate both of our unique circumstances, aiming for a fair distribution of household responsibilities. We have settled into what feels like a 70/30 split with me taking the majority of the household tasks and Charlie handling the rest. This is fair and manageable, without either of us feeling overwhelmed or resentful that one of us has more on their plate than the other. Most importantly, *we are responsible for our share, from start to finish*. That means I do not even think of the 30 percent of tasks that belong to Charlie. I do not make lists. I do not oversee. He gets them done because they are his; mercifully, no lists needed. And, in fairness, he doesn't oversee my tasks either.

We have been on a very long self-care journey of figuring out how to navigate this dynamic functionally in our marriage. Perhaps calling domestic partnership "self-care" sounds a bit weird to you, and if it does, I get it. Taking care of laundry, and dishes, and kids' school schedules hardly sounds as interesting as the cheap picture of self-care we see online and in the media—bubble baths, massages, puppy yoga, though yes, those things are lovely, wonderful *expressions* of self-care. But true self-care, the *act* of self-care, goes deeper than that. It involves showing up for ourselves; showing ourselves that our time is limited and important, that our contribution matters. For women, it means dismantling patriarchal ideas that convinced us that our time and labor are less valuable than a man's. It means forsaking our domestication.

But true self-care, the act of self-care, goes deeper than that. It involves showing up for ourselves; showing ourselves that our time is limited and important, that our contribution matters.

As I have stepped into this type of self-care, Charlie has come dutifully along with me. We work together now to divide our shared domestic tasks equitably, both the visible *and* the invisible tasks. I don't make lists because he has chosen to actively anticipate and take care of our household needs instead of passively receiving them from me. My sense of self-worth grows as I see my husband take tasks off my plate so that I can live a freer life and be less encumbered by the cage of domestic futility.

Charlie's self-worth is growing, too. His equitable participation in domestic labor has left me less exhausted and therefore more interested in sex and intimacy. With more time and energy on my hands, I am more capable of connecting with him in ways that deeply matter to him.

Impossibly, unthinkably, getting rid of the honey-do list and sharing the mental load has led to both of our core needs being met more fully than ever. I get my freedom, and Charlie gets his connection. And it's here, at this intersection of domestic labor and core needs—two things that are seemingly not related at all—that I realize how absolutely futile it is to navigate marriage without a firm commitment to self-care. I'm beginning to see that almost every issue that arises in marriage can be boiled down to a lack of self-care in one or both partners. When we stop advocating for ourselves, when we stop communicating our needs to the person who is supposed to love us most in the world, we betray ourselves. We betray our partners. We betray the little girl who's still inside us, begging for us to just *say what we need.*

When we stop advocating for ourselves, when we stop communicating our needs to the person who is supposed to love us most in the world, we betray ourselves. We betray our partners. We betray the little girl who's still inside us, begging for us to just say what we need.

Self-care, then, is choosing to speak up for ourselves—for that little girl who remembers how it's done. For me, that meant ripping up the honey-do list. It meant choosing partnership *with* my spouse over parenting *of* my spouse. Perhaps most importantly, this ongoing work has meant learning that my needs and wants are just as important as my husband's.

What I need matters, too.

Cultivate Your Truth Trench

- **Mental load is an actual load.** The invisible work of organizing, delegating, managing, and remembering household tasks is heavy. Do not listen to voices (including your own) who try to dismiss it or tell you it isn't that bad. The impact of mental load on individuals, particularly women, is significant, and self-care means expecting to share the load.
- **Gender stereotypes have served to subjugate women.** Part of the hard work of self-care in a patriarchal culture is challenging traditional gender roles and stereotypes surrounding household responsibilities. It's time to embrace the truth that both partners in a relationship are equally capable of managing domestic tasks and should share the burden of mental load regardless of their gender.
- **You deserve equitable partnership.** Advocate for equitable partnership, where both you and your partner take full responsibility for managing household tasks, decision-making, and planning. Reject the notion that one partner should passively receive tasks while the other manages and delegates them.
- **The only kind of self-care that can nourish is the kind that acts.** Bubble baths and facials are wonderful ways to relax and reset, but they will never bring fulfillment. Nourishing self-care is hard work: having the difficult conversations, setting boundaries, speaking needs. These are the things that nourish.

Chapter Nine

The Power of *Too*

I am a progressive-leaning feminist who was raised by conservative Baptists. I have spent most of my years defiantly pushing back against traditional gender roles that shove women out of the board room and into the kitchen. I knew that I would one day become a mom, but I also knew that nothing would stop me from chasing down the career of my dreams. I would *not* be a housewife as long as I could help it.

But when my firstborn finally came along in 2016, I felt some old vestiges of my Southern Baptist upbringing rising up in me. Growing up, my dad worked and my mom stayed home with me until I was well into my teenage years. I was grateful to have my mom home with me, and to this day I cherish the memories we made all those years at home together. That's what good Christian families do, right? As I thought back on my childhood and considered what's best for my own children, I wondered if it would be fair or appropriate for me to go to work every day while my kids were at daycare or with a nanny. My mom put her career on hold as long as it took to get me to an age where I could mostly take care of myself. Why wasn't I doing the same?

I was working as an executive at a tech startup when I became a mom. I loved the job, but it was demanding and had long hours—hours I just didn't feel right about taking away from my children (or, at the time, my only child). So, after having some hard conversations with Charlie, I decided to quit my job and become a stay-at-home mom.

I had hoped that staying home with my kids would fulfill me. I would magically forget my career ambitions and find satisfaction in being a full-time mom instead. But it didn't take long for me to understand how absolutely unrealistic that was. I was born with big dreams and the wingspan to reach them, but it felt like motherhood had put me in a cage. Grounded. No longer able to fly.

As a way to compromise between my career ambitions and my desire to be with my kids, I found ways to work while getting to spend most of my time at home. I started my own online retail store called The Sensible Mama, where I sold the top name brands in the baby industry. It was a job I could do at home for the most part, and when it grew too big for me to handle alone, I bought a warehouse and hired employees. My role in that business continued to be something I could do from home.

I started a YouTube channel, did freelance consulting work for big and small name brands, and began writing a book. In no time, I was a pretty busy gal. And for the last seven years, I have maintained that pace.

There was a time, several years ago, when all of this was too much for me to bear. I was spread too thin between my work, the kids, and the house, and I was drowning. Back then, I didn't feel like I was allowed to ask Charlie to help make sure I had time for my career. His career paid the bills while mine only supplemented our income.

I decided that it was wrong to ask him to sacrifice his valuable work schedule to make room for mine. And, as you've learned by this point in the book, that led to all the anger and resentment that eventually resulted in our separation.

Since the time that Charlie and I chose to reconcile our marriage, I have resolved to insist on my career being a priority just like his. He is still the "breadwinner" of our household (God, do I hate that term), so there are certainly some limits to how much time he is able to give when it comes to the kids and the house. The old me thought that it was unfair to ask him to make space for my career when so much of our financial stability was on his shoulders. To be fair, even the new me recognizes that (as we discussed in the last chapter) his career offers more tangible, practical value than mine, and that has to be taken into account.

The difference between the old me and the new me is that I finally understand that *my time is valuable, too, damn it*. My career might not bring in as much money as his does right now, but I still have ambitions and obligations. I still bring in a paycheck. The new, therapy-enhanced, self-care-committed me understands that even if things can't be "me, first," they at least need to be "me, too." I deserve for my time to matter and for us to make space for my career, *too*.

The difference between the old me and the new me is that I finally understand that *my time is valuable, too, damn it.*

As a matter of fact, even if I didn't have a career, my time would still matter, *too*. I'm lookin' at you, stay-at-home moms. Don't think I'm about to leave you out of this conversation. Just because you don't bring in a paycheck, that doesn't mean your time isn't valuable. Did you know that economists have estimated that your market value—if you were actually *paid* for the labor you provide—would be somewhere between $37,000 and $184,000 per year? So, yeah, your time has real-world, real monetary value, *too.* And since your job requires you to be on call 24/7, you are just as deserving as anyone else to have your spouse hold space for your time, *too.* Whatever it is—starting a hobby, going to yoga, writing a book—you deserve nonnegotiable, consistent, reliable time for yourself, *too.*

Whether we need time to focus on our careers, our personal ambitions, or simply on having some godforsaken peace and quiet, we all deserve for our spouses to hold space for that. There is no version of self-care that doesn't insist on it.

Whether we need time to focus on our careers, our personal ambitions, or simply on having some godforsaken peace and quiet, we all deserve for our spouses to hold space for that. There is no version of self-care that doesn't insist on it.

Since our reconciliation, Charlie and I have worked hard to make sure I get that time for my career. It has involved some negotiations and some creative thinking, but we've made it happen. The first thing I asked for was to have one day a week when I am not responsible for getting the kids ready for school and transporting them there. Monday through Thursday, I am responsible for those tasks. I get three hours of work time after the last drop-off and before the first pick up, and on those days, it's just enough to get my most pressing tasks done. But on Friday, Charlie gets up with the kids and begins their morning routine—feeding breakfast, making lunches, getting them dressed. He brings me a cup of coffee while I stay in bed and work. It's one blessed, glorious day a week when I get to drink my coffee before it goes cold. Because he handles the transportation of both kids, I get a full day of unbroken work time. I use that time to batch-prepare work for the following week so that I can make the most of my shorter workdays.

The next thing I asked was for Charlie to take over the responsibilities with the kids at 5:00 PM. I am in charge from the time they are home from school until 5:00, and after that, Charlie's in charge. He gets their dinner while I ride my Peloton, tie up loose ends from the workday, and get a shower.

Another thing I asked for was having a few hours each weekend to work and telling Charlie to do the same. On Saturdays and Sundays, we each get a two-hour chunk of "free range" time when the other parent handles the kids. It's our time to do whatever we want—work, shop, exercise, nap, whatever feels right. It allows us to make time for ourselves on the weekend and also helps the weekends pass by faster.

These small concessions have made a world of difference for my mental health and overall well-being. They have helped us both more effectively divide the household work and childcare and have given me a routine that I can count on. Essentially, these little guidelines put limits around my responsibilities with the house and kids, giving me clear "clock out" times. I need that structure. I deserve it.

I wish I could erase the training given to so many of us women, the training that told us we are supposed to be martyrs for our families. I wish we had never learned that we are supposed to make life easier for our husbands because "they are the breadwinners." Our contribution to the household is just as valuable as theirs, even if we aren't bringing in as much

I wish I could erase the training given to so many of us women, the training that told us we are supposed to be martyrs for our families.

tangible monetary value. Those contributions deserve to be appreciated. We need to be allowed to prioritize our work, our peace, and our well-being. We deserve for our needs to matter, too.

Too. Such a big word, packed into one tiny syllable.

Because I live and love inside a family, things can't always be *me, first*. That's not possible, or even realistic. But self-care is insisting on *me, too*. I will always make much of my family. I will never stop doing my best to take care of my kids and my dear husband, Charlie.

And I will take care of me. *Too*.

Cultivate Your Truth Trench

- **Establish priorities that serve you.** Reflect on your beliefs and assess if they align with your current values and aspirations. Give yourself permission to pursue your own desires and goals, even if they challenge traditional roles.
- **Strive for creativity in compromise.** It's so easy to become entrenched in gendered expectations about how to manage your household. Remember that there are many ways to keep a home afloat. Self-care is letting your partner know that you expect them to think creatively and outside the box to find compromises that allow you both to pursue your needs.
- **Your schedule works for you, not the other way around.** Implement routines and structures that work for you, that support your mental health and overall well-being. Establishing "clock out" times for household and childcare responsibilities can provide much-needed structure and balance in your life. Your schedule should relieve your stress, not add to it.
- **Your time is worth a damn.** Recognize the worth of your time, whether you're a stay-at-home parent or pursuing a career. Your contributions, whether monetary or not, are significant and deserve acknowledgment and support from your partner. Frankly, they deserve acknowledgment and support from you, too.

SECTION II

Girls Brunch:

Self-Care in Friendships

Chapter Ten

Crabs in a Bucket

We need to talk about the importance of self-care inside our friendships. But first, we have to talk about crabs.

There is this thing that crabs do if you put them in a bucket. Inside the bucket is starvation and, eventually, death. Outside the bucket is freedom and safety. And although the crabs are physically able to climb out of the bucket, none of them try.

It's not that there are no crabs who possess the desire to get out of the bucket. It's that whenever those brave crabs try to scale the wall and flee to safety, their peers at the bottom reach up and yank them back down. *Every time.*

And eventually, even the bravest crabs stop trying.

Now they sit, starving at the bottom of the bucket with the crabs who didn't have the guts to try. Those intrepid, extraordinary crabs now look no different than the rest. Doomed to a fate they didn't deserve. Suddenly, unremarkable.

This bizarre behavior is what scientists call crab theory. It's the idea that although any of the crabs could easily climb out of the bucket, their resistance toward seeing another crab do it first leads to the demise of them all. They would rather see the entire group crushed and starved than allow one to get out and survive.

As I'm sure you've already guessed, this behavior doesn't just apply to crabs.

I am thirty-eight years old at the time of writing this book. I have been in lots of buckets, with lots of different crabs. Although the buckets have changed in size and shape, and the crabs in my company have come and gone, one thing has never changed: there are *scale-the-wall crabs*, and there are *yank-you-down crabs*.

I am a scale-the-wall crab. I always will be.

My time in buckets has taught me that the crabs I choose to surround myself with really matter. I need to be with other scale-the-wall crabs. The yank-you-down crabs have come dangerously close to getting me crushed or fit for someone's plate.

The beauty of our friends is that we get to choose them. Our choices matter because eventually, we're going to end up in a bucket with them. When we find ourselves in those dark and scary places, where freedom isn't far but it's a big vertical climb, we need the right friends in the bucket with us.

I want the kind of friends who encourage me to reach. The kind who cheer me on as I make my ascent, who pick me up and dust me off when I fall and tell me to try again.

I want the kind of friends who encourage me to reach. The kind who cheer me on as I make my ascent, who pick me up and dust me off when I fall and tell me to try again. I want them to celebrate for me when I get to the top, even if it means they can't quite get there yet themselves. I want them to trust that when they are ready, I will be back at the top of the bucket, extending a hand to pull them out. They know their time will come because they are scale-the-wall crabs, too.

I'm finally learning how to find and keep those friends, which I'll talk about in the next chapter. For now, I want to talk about *not* those friends.

Maybe I'm wrong here, but I have a feeling many of us have had more experiences with the bad friends, the *yank-you-down* friends, than the *scale-the-wall* friends. These are the folks who call themselves friends—who perhaps even, to some degree, actually think of themselves as our friends—but who never seem to show up for us the way a true friend would. If we're being honest with ourselves, we have probably known for a while that they don't belong in our lives. We just don't really know how to part ways. We grapple with guilt. We gaslight ourselves and wonder if maybe we're being unfair, maybe they deserve another chance.

It doesn't help matters that those friends tend to be very good in the art of gaslighting, too. They know they will never leave the bucket, so to speak. They will not try to elevate themselves out of circumstances they don't like. They won't take care of their mental health, won't go to therapy. They won't do the hard work of personal growth and self-care that you are doing, and they won't be accountable for their own mistakes. They prefer the deadly comfort of the bottom of the bucket over the fresh air of freedom at the top.

Your efforts to get out of the bucket force them to face their own shortcomings. They could let you go, free to chase down greatness, but they would rather keep you in the bucket by their side. After all, if you never escape the bucket, then it's okay that they never do, either.

So, they gaslight you to make you stay. They tell you that you are the problem. They call your ambition *greed*. Your personal growth *pretentiousness*. Your self-care *selfish*. They tell you that they yank you back down because they want to keep you safe. *They're just looking out for you.* How dare you leave them behind?

Because you're a good person who is willing to self-reflect, you wonder if perhaps they're right. So, you stay, choosing an unkindness to yourself over an unkindness to them. And with that, all your talent, all your gifts, all the unique and sparkling things that make you, *you*, wither away with them at the bottom of the bucket.

We simply can't afford to have those kinds of friends. There is too much at stake, too much to lose. Our time and energy are limited and deserve to be spent on friends who enrich and encourage us. Self-care in our friendships, then, means learning the difficult skill of walking away from friends who don't. After all, I'd argue that those people aren't really our friends anyway.

We simply can't afford to have those kinds of friends. There is too much at stake, too much to lose. Our time and energy are limited and deserve to be spent on friends who enrich and encourage us.

Over the years, I have painstakingly learned this art. It's never been fun, but it has gotten easier with practice. I have gotten really good at identifying certain types of yank-you-down, bottom-of-the-bucket friends with a quickness and doing my best to keep them at bay:

- **The Crisis Friend**, who only calls when they are in crisis (which is often) and who never asks how you are doing.
- **The Envy Friend**, who never seems to be happy for your good news.
- **The Weirdly Competitive Friend**, who sees themselves in competition with you for literally no reason.

- **The One-Way-Street Friend**, who constantly drains your cup and never fills it back up. Oh, and don't forget,
- **The "Friend-Zoned Friend,"** who feels entitled to romance or sex from you and thinks you've done them an unfairness by offering friendship instead.

It can be hard to cut ties with these friends, especially if we have known them for a long time or have let them make us feel responsible for their well-being. But if we don't want to share their fate at the bottom of the bucket, we have to get climbing. We will always hope that they will one day decide to leave the bucket themselves, but that is up to them. It can't be our responsibility. Self-care is accepting the uncomfortable truth that we have to be choosy about who we give our time and energy to.

I will always extend my hand to a fellow scale-the-wall crab. I will also love myself enough to leave behind the ones who are content to stay inside the bucket. I can wish them well, and hope that they never end up served on someone's plate. I just can't make them want out of the bucket. Only they can do that.

Self-care in friendships means sincerely rooting for even the crabs who would drag me down, but doing so from outside the bucket. Put into practice, that mindset looks like this:

- I am not a bad person for leaving people behind who do not support or enrich my life.
- I am not responsible for saving those people.
- I can wish the best for the people who would rather stay in the bucket.
- But I am of better use to the world on the outside of the bucket.

Cultivate Your Truth Trench

- **Don't get in buckets with the wrong crabs.** You will meet many crabs. Some of them are scale-the-wall crabs, and others are yank-you-down crabs. Do your best to stay away from the latter.
- **You deserve friends who want to see you succeed.** Surround yourself with friends who uplift and support your ambitions and growth rather than those who drag you down with their own insecurities.
- **You can't save people from themselves.** Accept that you are not responsible for saving friends who choose to remain in toxic patterns, and acknowledge that it's okay to prioritize your own well-being by letting go of such friendships.
- **Root for others from a safe distance.** Practice genuine empathy by wishing the best for friends who may hold you back, but recognize that you can better serve both yourself and the world by moving forward without them.

Chapter Eleven

Friendship Breakups

If there was ever a time that was ripe for friendship breakups, it was during the height of the pandemic. Something about being stuck inside our homes with nothing but our thoughts and the people in our COVID bubble really made us question what we were, and were not, willing to accept in our lives.

Now that I think about it, maybe it was the COVID bubbles themselves that triggered these questions. Perhaps many of us looked around at our lockdown buddies and asked ourselves, *If I had to do this all over again, are these the people I would want in my bubble?* The concept of bubbles was, until that time, a foreign concept to most of us. As lockdowns swept the country, we had to do something that many of us had never done in our lives—decide who belonged in our bubble and who did not. Political tensions heightened as we found ourselves divided over what to do about face coverings, vaccines, and group gatherings. We had to communicate our convictions on these issues and then see which of our friends felt the same. Friends who shared our convictions were welcomed into our bubble while, sadly, many of us had to temporarily cut ties with the friends who did not. It was perhaps the first time that many of us actually set boundaries in our friendships.

I don't know about you, but going through the meticulous process of forming my bubble did something to my brain chemistry. I emerged from the lockdown with a new attitude about my friendships. I've called a lot of people friends over the years, but having to define a small bubble of them made me realize that most of those people were just acquaintances. I was trying to show up as a friend to too many people, and most of those people weren't matching my energy, and because of the pandemic, I noticed it for the first time. An unexpected gift from our time in lockdown was that it forced us to take a look at our idea of friendship and give it a hard reset, redefine what it means, and make some changes.

We aren't very good at practicing self-care in our friendships, it seems. Maybe we have an anemic idea of friendships, and we fear that our friends won't stick around if we show up authentically, set boundaries, and communicate our needs. Maybe we would just rather avoid the confrontation in order to keep these fragile friendships. Maybe the real culprit is that we have watered down the definition of *friend* so significantly that we now count way too many people as friends. People who should be thought of as acquaintances, coworkers, or neighbors have been elevated to friend status, and with that comes the pressure to pour into them all the things we reserve for our friends. Things like being there to listen, taking on their burdens, and giving them more energy than we have to spare. If we would allow ourselves to reserve the label of *friend* for the people to whom it really applies, we would find it so much easier to take care of ourselves in our friendships. I bet we'd be better at

It is impossible to communicate our needs, to be vulnerable, to lay our souls bare, to set boundaries, and to invest deeply with all those people. We only have the capacity to show up authentically and energetically with a special few.

taking care of our friends, too. It is impossible to communicate our needs, to be vulnerable, to lay our souls bare, to set boundaries, and to invest deeply with all those people. We only have the capacity to show up authentically and energetically with a special few.

What we have to understand is that we are a limited resource. Our time, energy, emotional labor, and patience are not infinite, and we have to be intentional about how we dole them out. Perhaps one of the greatest acts of self-care we can take in the context of our friendships is having the courage and the self-compassion to let some of them go.

When I was in high school, a teacher said to me, "Amber, you are like a sprinkler. You sprinkle water everywhere but never enough in one place to count." His words stung at the time, but even after all these years, I have never forgotten them. I am thankful that he decided to deliver a painful truth instead of a convenient lie. I was spreading myself too thin, committing to more things than I could handle, and in my efforts to be the best at them all, I became good at none.

I think that this applies to our friendships, too. I want to be the kind of friend who sprinkles enough into my friends to count. No, I want to *pour* into my friends—to douse them in whatever goodness I have to offer. When I sprinkle into too many cups, I can't make a difference to any of them; worse, I end up with nothing left over for myself. So, over the last few years I have worked diligently to identify the friends I am willing and able to pour into and which ones I am not. I've also made sure that every person I'm pouring into is *also* pouring into me. Anyone who hasn't met those criteria has been either released or demoted.

I can't say that it was easy, but it was definitely worth it. Through a bit of trial and error, I have established some practical tips for these difficult friendship breakups, and I'm going to share them with you now. Remember that this is what worked for *me*, and it might not be what works for you. Take what resonates and apply it, and leave or modify the rest. This is your garden. I'm just here to lay the truth trenches.

First, remember that *clear is kind*. This is a mantra I learned to embrace after reading Melissa Urban's book *Boundaries*, which I highly recommend. Setting boundaries with friends doesn't have to be cruel, even if those boundaries mean goodbye. I can guarantee that the friends you want to step back from would rather you be honest about that than to let the friendship slowly fade. You can be firm *and* kind, and you can practice empathy and compassion as you honestly share how you feel.

Second, take time to decide which friendships you want to release completely and which friendships you might like to keep but in a new form. Be quick to release the "friends" who are toxic, selfish, cruel, competitive, or demanding. To those people, you don't owe an explanation unless you want to give one. Maybe the right decision is to just block them. Maybe it's to tell them why the friendship cannot move forward and then go no contact. Just remember that toxic people don't tend to take accountability when you express your feelings. However you decide to handle it, whatever you choose to say to those friends before closing the door should be purely for *you*. Decide what you

Be quick to release the "friends" who are toxic, selfish, cruel, competitive, or demanding. To those people, you don't owe an explanation unless you want to give one.

need to say in order to feel closure and say that. Don't hope for it to go anywhere past your final words.

The friends who aren't toxic might be willing to reexamine the friendship under new terms. In order for that to happen, you'll have to be really honest and up-front. I recently told a friend that I needed to take a step back from our friendship because I felt that she was depending too heavily on me for her emotional needs. I was becoming her external processor for all of her feelings, and it was too much and too often. I didn't have the emotional energy anymore. But she was a kind person, someone whom I deeply loved, so I explained to her that I wanted her in my life but that I just couldn't be her emotional support human anymore. And in order for our friendship to move forward, I also needed her to invest some of her energy into supporting me, too. It wasn't easy, but through clear and honest conversation, acknowledging each other's feelings, and setting boundaries, we established a new normal. You can do it, too. It just takes a commitment to being completely and unflinchingly honest.

Lastly, remember that these friends might not be okay with the new terms of the friendship. As you begin these conversations, go in with the understanding that some friends might choose to say goodbye instead of making the changes you ask for. I encourage you to think of it as them choosing to respect your boundaries in the only way they know how, with the only resources they have. They may not know how to be your friend without crossing your boundaries, so stepping back is the only thing they can do. Try not to take it personally.

I encourage you to think of it as them choosing to respect your boundaries in the only way they know how, with the only resources they have.

True self-care is prioritizing your peace and mental health, even over the peace and mental health of your friends. This is the important work of self-care. It's doing the hard, yet necessary things that bring fulfillment. Even if they are uncomfortable at first. Doing this hard work in your friendships can be an act of compassion if you choose to see it that way. Releasing friends who drain you and don't fill you back up frees them to find the people who do have the energy to invest in them. It also frees you to invest more deeply into the people who are truly your friends, to pour abundantly into their cups, and to allow them to pour into yours.

Letting go of friends who aren't enriching your life is a brave act of self-care. Continuing to invest time and energy in relationships that don't make you feel fulfilled can drain your emotional resources and leave you feeling empty. By releasing these friendships, you create space for new and healthier connections that keep you sustained and full. You can have your potato chips friends—ones who can bring you happiness in a pinch but who can't truly fill you up. Just make sure you're also finding and investing in the friends who truly nourish you.

Letting go of friends who aren't enriching your life is a brave act of self-care.

Cultivate Your Truth Trench

- **Acquaintances are not friends—you don't owe them the same effort.** Spreading yourself too thin across numerous relationships can dilute your impact and leave you feeling depleted. Be choosy about who you invest your time into.
- **Boundaries are for platonic relationships, too.** Recognize the importance of setting boundaries in friendships, understanding that it's crucial to reserve time and energy for those who reciprocate and uplift rather than drain our cups.
- **Sometimes, things change; sometimes, they end.** Not all friendships will withstand new terms or boundaries, so be prepared for the possibility of some friends choosing to part ways rather than adapt to changes.
- **It is scary, but it is brave.** Letting go of friendships that no longer serve you is an act of brave self-care, creating space for healthier connections that nourish and sustain you.

Chapter Twelve

The Dalai Lama

The only thing that sucks about friendship breakups is that sometimes they happen *to you.*

Just because we are working on showing up authentically, reaching our highest potential, going to therapy, and taking good care of our mental health, that doesn't mean that everyone who we call friends will call us friends in return. As they say, you can be the ripest, juiciest peach on the tree and there will still be people who don't like peaches.

In the years since the lockdowns lifted, I've had a couple of friends choose to break up with me. It's been hard to digest, despite the fact that I have done the same. Ego is a funny, tireless thing. I know that I didn't break up with friends because I hated them or because they were terrible people (at least most of them weren't). I did it because I was out of time, out of energy, out of spoons. I should have easily understood that the friends who decided to part ways with me did it for the same reasons.

But nah. Not this gal. Obviously, they hate me, and I'm a terrible person, and it's only a matter of time until everyone else sees I'm terrible, too. One friend breaking up with me is the domino that will bring all the rest down.

Of course that's not true, but the truth doesn't always matter when our hearts are hurting.

If you've been broken up with by a friend or are going through a breakup with a friend right now, I know how bad it hurts. I know you're suffering. And if your friend did the breakup badly by leaving you in the dark and slowly fading into the distance, you are also very disoriented and confused. I want you to know that it's normal to feel that way. I also want to share with you the only thing that I think can give comfort. And it's from the mouth of the Dalai Lama.

During my separation from Charlie, while I was consuming self-help books like they were five-star cuisine, I came across a copy of *The Art of Happiness* by the Dalai Lama and Howard Cutler in a local used bookstore. I was desperately unhappy and figured that if anyone could show me how to be happy again, it was the Dalai Lama himself.

One of the most important takeaways I got from the book was that the basic premise and purpose of life is to seek happiness. If you were raised in a Western, Christian household like I was, that statement might hit your ears wrong. Many of us were raised to believe that happiness is the *opposite* of the purpose of life. It sounds like sacrilege to hear that our chief purpose in life is just to be happy. But according to Buddhist teachings, it is true. Seeking happiness is not self-centered, self-indulgent, or plain old self*ish*. It is, in fact, our most basic human purpose.

Seeking happiness is not self-centered, self-indulgent, or plain old *selfish*. It is, in fact, our most basic human purpose.

When I think of friends I've lost, it's easy to think that their disinterest in having me in their life was about *me*. But the real reason they chose to cut ties with me isn't about me at all. It's about them, plain and simple. The reason they abandoned me is that they are searching for their ultimate happiness. They are in pursuit of whatever they feel is best for them, as defined by them.

In *The Art of Happiness*, the authors claim that the decisions people make in life are less about *moving away* from something bad and more about *moving toward* something that they think is good. I don't know about you, but to me this difference in meaning is profound. It means that I can choose not to see friendship breakups as a judgment of my value or worth. If a friend chooses not to have me in their life anymore, it is not because I have some deficit of worth or that I am unlikeable. It means that, according to *that specific person*, I do not provide what they believe will lead to their happiness. It has nothing to do with me. It's entirely about them and their needs.

This can be especially true if the friend who is breaking up with me has a different objective for our friendship than I have. Let's say that someone likes being my friend because they want to become an influencer and I have the experience and connections to help them get started. I, on the other hand, like being their friend because we have a lot in common and we seem to sincerely like each other. Then one day, I decide I'm done with social media. I deactivate all of my accounts and focus on me and my family instead. Suddenly, to that friend who thought my ability to open doors would lead to her ultimate happiness in the pursuit of her dreams, I have no more worth.

To her.

Our friendship fizzles, then fades. I hear from her less frequently, then not at all. And I'm left feeling confused, abandoned, and worthless.

Has anything about my worth actually changed? No. In fact, at least according to my own pursuit of happiness, my value has gone up. I've made a positive decision for my own mental health and well-being and shown myself that I am worthy of self-care. But to my friend, I have suddenly lost my value because I no longer possess the tools to help *her* reach happiness. It may still hurt to lose a friend that way, but it's not about me. It says nothing about me at all.

I can already hear the question you're aching to ask. *But Amber, what about when a friend breaks up with me because they explicitly say it's about me? When they say something about me makes them not want to be friends anymore?*

Honestly? My argument still stands.

A few years ago, a friend of mine suddenly began giving me the cold shoulder. She stopped responding to my text messages, wouldn't take my calls. The rare times I did hear from her she was cold and distant, treating me like a piece of gum she stepped in. For months, I chased her, desperate to understand what had changed so suddenly and desperate for a balm to soothe the ache of unexplained rejection. Then one day, I finally confronted her. I couldn't keep hanging on; I just needed to know what in God's name had happened.

Our conversation was bizarre. She was aggressive and cruel, snarling at me as she spoke. She told me that she didn't have room for me in her life anymore because I am weak, dumb, and powerless. She said that I portray myself as so smart and strong online but that in person I am dim and ineffectual—the exact opposite of who I say I am.

Even if she was right (she wasn't), and even if I was dim and ineffectual (I'm not), it wouldn't change the fact that it *wasn't about me.* In *her* estimation, someone *like me*, regardless of whether her estimation was correct, couldn't push her toward her idea of happiness.

I was a peach, and she no longer liked peaches.

We can't control other people's taste. We can't control how they choose to perceive us. It's easy to think we can, and that's what compels us to chase them when they step back or withdraw their approval of us. We want to argue, to persuade, and to convince them that they are wrong about us. We do this because, sadly, we have placed our sense of worth and value in their fickle hands.

We can't control other people's taste. We can't control how they choose to perceive us.

How easily we hand our self-worth over to others, how we marvel in the way they delicately handle it at first. As long as they take good care of our worth, we feel worthy.

Sometimes, those people turn out to be not the people we thought they were or who they portrayed themselves to be. Other times, they just evolve and want different things and people—a different route to happiness. When that happens, and they discard our precious self-worth like a grease-covered hamburger wrapper, we feel worthless.

This is why, my darling friend, we don't plant our worth in someone else's garden. Self-care is planting our worth in our own garden, where we can watch over it, cultivate it, and let it blossom and grow. When we have ownership over our self-worth, when it has grown deep roots, the changing weather patterns of our friendships can never drown it out. It is immune to their rejection or scorn. We don't chase when they leave because although we may miss them, they haven't run off with our worth.

This is why, my darling friend, we don't plant our worth in someone else's garden.

Self-care in our friendships is knowing with our entire soul that other people's feelings about us have nothing to do with us. Our worth is immutable, unchangeable, unaffected by the whims of friends. It is always with us, and it doesn't change just because someone else says so.

You are wildly, overwhelmingly worthy.

Plant that truth, and let it take root.

Cultivate Your Truth Trench

- **It's about them, not about you.** A friend's decision to end the relationship is often about their own pursuit of happiness, not a reflection of your worth. It's about their needs and objectives, not your deficiencies.
- **Rejection doesn't define you.** Even if a friend explicitly blames you for the breakup, it's essential to remember that their perception doesn't define your worth. Their rejection is about their preferences, not your intrinsic value.
- **Don't entrust your worth to others.** Placing your self-worth in the hands of others is risky. Self-care involves cultivating and nurturing your self-worth internally, independent of others' opinions or actions.
- **Your worth is immutable.** Remember, regardless of the ebbs and flows of friendships, you are inherently and undeniably worthy. Plant this truth within yourself and let it flourish.

Chapter Thirteen

At the Table

Have you ever thought about whether you have the right people at your table? It's a metaphor my therapist and I often use to help me sort out who belongs in a seat of prominence in my life and who doesn't.

The table is our inner sanctum. Much like the depiction of Jesus at the Last Supper, surrounded by His twelve disciples who knew Him best, our table represents our life and the people we trust to have an influence on it.

It's not unkind to say that some people belong at our table and some do not. The undeniable reality of life is that although we can sit at an infinite number of *other people's tables*, we have a limited number of seats at our own. This means that we need to carefully choose who occupies those seats. And I don't know about you, but I have spent a lot of time giving those seats away to *anyone* who would sit in them.

I am a chronic people pleaser, but I'm working on that—a people pleaser in recovery, if you will. I often view myself as less interesting, successful, or useful than other people. I have a hard time understanding why anyone would *want* a seat at my table. Because of that, whenever someone comes along who does seem interested in one of those seats, I give it away easily.

Exuberantly.

I've been fortunate, by sheer luck, to accumulate dozens of great friends and advisors in those seats over the years, people who encourage me, uplift me, cheer me on—the *scale-the-wall* crabs who want to see me succeed because they want to succeed, too. I've also had the misfortune of gathering my fair share of *yank-you-down* crabs at my table: people who bring negativity, toxicity, and drama to my life, people who don't share my values (although many of them pretended to at first), or who don't have my best interest at heart, and people who are judgmental, critical, or unsupportive and who bring more harm than good to my life.

With lots of therapy, I've been learning how to undo the people-pleasing ways that "helped" me assemble all those bad crabs at my table. The first step was the hardest and loneliest of all because it meant clearing the table altogether. It meant pushing everyone out of the room and taking the seat at the head of the table—the place of prominence—where I had not sat in a very long time.

It meant getting comfortable, at least for a while, with being alone.

It meant getting comfortable, at least for a while, with being alone.

Removing their chatter from my table and my mind allowed me to think, perhaps for the first time in years, about what I truly need in order to feel loved and supported. Little by little, I began assigning one of my core needs to every seat. Like arranging the seating chart for wedding guests before they arrive, I placed little mental place cards at every seat. *This friend will meet this need. This friend will meet that one.* Of course, I knew I would have friends who didn't meet any of those particular needs, and that was okay. We can allow ourselves to have "standing room only" friends who don't fill a core need but whom we like having around anyway. I just knew that if I could get a core group of friends at my table who each met a need that mattered to me, I would find real self-actualization and fulfillment. I'd probably be a lot happier in my friendships, too.

After all, even the fairy-tale maidens had a posse of their own. Snow White had the seven dwarfs. Cinderella and Sleeping Beauty had the fairy godmothers. It's as if even the storytellers of old always knew that a girl needs more than her prince. She needs some kick-ass companions to be her mentors, her guides, her unfailing friends.

So, I set about identifying the different roles that I wanted friends to fulfill in my life. In what areas of my life would I want love and support, and perhaps more importantly, how would those friends *enrich me* in those areas? What contribution could they make to my physical, mental, emotional, or spiritual well-being? I envisioned myself as the indomitable Captain Planet from my youth, and my friends were the Planeteers whose unique superpowers made me into the mega-charged superhero I was born to be.

I'm going to share with you what powers I wanted *my* Planeteers, the esteemed friends at *my* table, to have. Just remember that this is a highly personal thing. You may need totally different types of friends at your table, and that's okay. Think of this as a template to follow—an example that you can pull from, build upon, and personalize.

Across the board, I knew I needed all the friends at my table to be working at least as hard on their personal development as I am working on mine. The people at my table would be the ones who would see *all of my shit*, the good and the bad, and I didn't want people who weren't working on their own shit to be looking at my shit. I didn't need them all to be in therapy, necessarily, but I did need them all to have a dedicated interest in their own healing and personal growth and to be taking active steps to move toward those things. No one would be considered for access to my table if they weren't doing that work.

I needed someone to be my *ride-or-die friend*. Forgive the imagery, but I just needed that bestie who would bury a body with me if it came down to it. As the friend who currently occupies that seat has said (and she's had that seat for over twenty years), "I wouldn't just bury the body for you; I'd feed it to the pigs." Yes, it's gross. But that's a ride-or-die for you.

I live most of my adult life very publicly online, so I needed a *social media hygiene friend*. This would be someone who also knows what it's like to live transparently in front of millions of people every day and the toll that takes on your mental health. The internet is brutal. I needed someone who understood.

Faith is a big part of my life, but I am walking through a season of deconstruction. I am working on releasing the beliefs that were handed down to me from my parents and embracing my own beliefs instead. It is a lonely road, a bewildering road, and the stakes are high. I needed a *spiritual friend* who could witness my journey and provide equal measures of grace and truth.

I needed a *sage friend* who was perhaps a bit older than me and who I trusted to help me make wise decisions when I didn't know what to do, a friend who I could count on to tell the truth even when it's not what I want to hear. In addition, I needed a *polar opposite friend* who shared my values but whose instincts were usually different than mine, as well as an *out of the comfort zone friend* who could nudge (or shove) me toward my goals when I doubted myself. Lastly, I needed a *let your hair down friend* whose friendship was simple, uncomplicated, and fun.

Altogether, seven seats at my table: seven friends, seven Planeteers, seven fairy godmothers. When I realized that my list had, by chance, stopped at seven, I couldn't help smiling with satisfaction. Seven is a number that represents completeness, perfection. By consciously recognizing my own needs for friendship, I'd unconsciously imagined a complete, perfect table of friends.

I have spent the last year finding those people. It's taken a lot of false starts and dashed hopes. It's required me to move people out of their seats swiftly when I realized they weren't enriching my life, or worse, were actually doing me harm. It's meant being comfortable with seats sitting empty while I find the right person to fill them. Slowly, painstakingly, I have begun finding my people. I have discovered how much easier it is to take good care of myself when I have the right people at my table.

I have discovered how much easier it is to take good care of myself when I have the right people at my table.

Whatever the "right people" look like for you, whichever needs you are looking to have met, here are some traits that I think are crucial for anyone who sits at your table. First, there needs to be *safety* between you and them. There needs to be a sense that you can bring good news, bad news, and even constructive criticism to each other and know that the friendship is safe. Safety means knowing that you both value the friendship over any disagreement or difference of opinion and that you can speak your mind freely without risking the loss of the friendship (within reason).

Second, you need *trust*. These friends will be your guides and mentors. They will be the ones to whom you hold up difficult decisions, to whom you come when you are at a crossroads and need their advice. You need to know that they will be honest with you—willing even to hurt your feelings if it means helping you make the right decisions for yourself. And if there is *safety* as discussed earlier, it's much easier for them to trust that they can do that. It's also easier for you to trust that they have your best interest at heart even if you don't like what they have to say.

Lastly, you need *mutual regard for each other's best interest*. Do the friends at your table have your best interest at heart? Would they offer up a shoulder to boost you out of the bucket, even if it meant they couldn't get out themselves? Would they know that you would come back for them, because you love them the way they love you? The right friends are not afraid to see you succeed. They don't fear it because there is safety, trust, and mutual affection. They know that your success is their success, or at least that it will lead to their success eventually. Your fulfillment is theirs, too.

The right friends are not afraid to see you succeed.

Love yourself wildly enough to seek the friendships that nourish, enrich, and satisfy. Self-care that does not include a willingness to hunt for those friendships is useless. Have the courage, the audacity, to excuse the folks from your table who would rather upturn your plate than watch you eat.

Love yourself enough to seek the friends you deserve, *who deserve you in return*—all of the sparkling, sacred, radiant, remarkable *you*.

Cultivate Your Truth Trench

- **The seats at your table are sacred.** Reflect on the people in your life and consider whether they truly belong at your table—the inner circle of influence and trust. It's essential to recognize who enriches your life and who may bring negativity and toxicity. Sometimes, clearing the table completely is necessary to reassess and rebuild.
- **Seek friends who take care of their own well-being.** Surround yourself with friends who are actively engaged in personal development and growth. This ensures that they understand your journey and can provide meaningful support without judgment.
- **You deserve safety, trust, and mutual regard.** The foundation of any friendship at your table should include these three things. These qualities foster an environment where you can freely express yourself and receive honest feedback and support.
- **Love yourself enough.** Self-care involves seeking friendships that nourish and satisfy your soul. Have the courage to let go of toxic friendships and seek friends who uplift and celebrate you for who you are.

SECTION III

Kitchen Table:

Self-Care in Families

Chapter Fourteen

The Missing Village

Was my mom this lonely when she was raising me?

It's a question I have pondered a lot since becoming a mom. My memories of my mother are sparkling and fun. I was her only child and easily her whole world. My dad worked long hours as an air traffic controller, and we didn't have family around. Living in an ultra-rural community in southern Georgia where neighbors could be miles apart from one another also meant she didn't have much social support around her, apart from perhaps a few church friends whom she saw at Sunday School. She didn't seem to mind, at least not from my limited perspective. We played together, laughed together, had afternoon snacks together. She was my best friend—my only friend for those first many years—and she made my life feel so full. How could she feel lonely when she had me?

Looking back now, through the eyes of an adult instead of a little kid who adored her mommy, I think I see a glimpse of what those years were like for her. She never showed me any sign of it, of course, but I see it now. The loneliness that was there, just behind her smiling eyes.

She had my dad, but because of his rotating schedule and demanding hours, he was gone a lot. When he was home, he was often sleeping off a midnight shift. And because they had made the difficult decision to separate me from my extended family to break a cycle of addiction (more on that in the following chapters), that also meant she didn't have her family around to lend a hand or a hug. So, for the most part, my mom just had me to fill her days.

She was *so alone*.

Now, as a mom in my thirties, my heart aches for her. It aches because it understands. It comprehends her silent suffering, her invisible labor.

At one time, our families were situated within communities. In these communities, mothers could find caregivers to help with the child-rearing, the housekeeping, the moral lessons. Children were raised by not just their parents but also their grandparents, aunts and uncles, and older cousins. Neighbors knew one another and often lent a helping hand. We said *it takes a village*, and we meant it. Raising children, and all the tasks that entails, was treated not as the sole responsibility of the parents but rather as the collective responsibility of the entire community. This was a wonderful way of life for children because it created a sense of belonging and of common good. But it seems, at least in my opinion, that the people who benefited most from the village mentality were the parents. Particularly the moms.

Moms, in many ways, are more isolated than ever. Having no village to share in the daily responsibilities of child-rearing, moms these days are expected to be everything at once.

Sadly, the village is no more.

Moms, in many ways, are more isolated than ever. Having no village to share in the daily responsibilities of child-rearing, moms these days are expected to be everything at once. They are nannies, chefs, playmates, spiritual teachers, instructors in morality, diaper changers, snack getters, chauffeurs, bath givers, school lunch packers, the deliverers of discipline, and the providers of comfort. They are expected to keep up with pediatrician visits, dentist appointments, and regular haircuts. They should serve on the PTA, volunteer for field trips, and make treats for the class on their child's birthday.

On top of all these expectations, moms are supposed to take good care of their bodies, eat right, and exercise. Get the baby weight off. Get their libido back. Be a domestic goddess in the kitchen and a sex goddess in the bedroom. Take care of aging parents, check in on ailing relatives, and be responsible for addicted or maladjusted siblings. They have a world of expectations on their shoulders and almost no one to help them lift the load.

I see my own mom in a whole new light these days. I see a woman who was tossing life preservers to the people she loved while letting the current slowly pull her under. In a way, I am her. We all are.

We need the expectations of women to catch up with our new, village-less society. Until then, I think it's up to us to make our own villages. There are ways of building a village of support around ourselves, and I'd like to show you how. But before I do, I need to address the reality of privilege. Although many types of self-care are accessible to everyone because they are *internal* processes like building self-esteem, building your own village is a privilege that not everyone has. It requires tangible resources. It means having money to hire people to take work off our plates or having a support system of family or friends to trade and share resources with. Not everyone has access to these things, so I proceed with caution, understanding that for some people these tips will be practical, and for others, they will be aspirational.

For those with the financial resources to hire help around the house or with the kids, allow me to give you official permission to use them. I've spoken to the committee. We all approve.

For those with the financial resources to hire help around the house or with the kids, allow me to give you official permission to use them. I've spoken to the committee. We all approve.

I don't know when it became dishonorable for moms to hire out their heaping pile of responsibilities to other people, but it's time to let that self-handicapping belief go. You are not a lazy wife or a disinterested mom for wanting to hire someone to vacuum your floors or take your kids to the park. I know it's easy to feel guilty about paying someone to do something that you could do for free, but try thinking about it like this: how much money is one hour of your time worth?

I have a number in my head of what an hour of my time is worth. I came up with this number by asking myself, "How much money would someone have to pay me to do [insert chore or task] for an hour instead of doing something that could actually make me money or bring me or my family joy?" Anything that would cost less than that amount of money to pay someone else to do, I'm paying them to do it. This frees me up to do things that earn money, that fulfill me, or that help me make memories with my family and friends. This is a mindset I've loosely adapted from Tim Ferris's book *The 4-Hour Work Week*, which I highly recommend if you have the time (it's a rather hefty read).

This is sensible self-care. It is not selfish. It is not irresponsible. It is using your resources to buy the support that we used to get for free when we had villages to help us.

This is sensible self-care. It is not selfish. It is not irresponsible. It is using your resources to buy the support that we used to get for free when we had villages to help us.

If hiring help is out of reach for you, there are practical ways to trade and share resources with friends or neighbors that can have the same effect.

If you have neighbors whose kids attend the same school as yours, try organizing a carpooling system so that you take turns doing the chauffeuring. It's amazing how much time and mental energy you can save just by not having to sit in car line a few days a week. You can do babysitting swaps, which are one of my favorite perks of village building. Get together with friends or neighbors who also have kids and rotate who babysits all the children on a Friday or Saturday night. It's free childcare from people you trust, and you get at least one weekend a month for a guaranteed date night. Another cool idea is to make community freezer meals. Each person in your little self-made village makes a big batch of freezer meals, and you divide them up among one another. That way, everyone only cooks one meal but gets a variety of meals to use throughout the week.

I recently heard of single moms renting apartments together and living as a cohabitating family, pooling their resources and co-parenting the children. There are also communes popping up around the country that provide childcare, education, and professional development courses for young or single moms. This is top-tier village building!

It's so easy to lean into the loneliness and the exhaustion, the sheer overwhelm, of parenting in a culture that has forgotten the power of villages. We are expected to parent as effectively as women did when villages were around while having none of the support.

The time may be more crucial than ever for us to build our own villages. Taking

The time may be more crucial than ever for us to build our own villages.

good care of ourselves means acknowledging that we can't do it alone because *we were never meant to*. It means giving ourselves permission to lean on one another, maybe even to depend on one another. It means saying yes to help when it is offered and offering help generously and often because we understand the struggle. In some cases, it means choosing unconventional living arrangements that can give us the support we need.

Yes, people will judge. They will criticize. I am convinced that the world hates few things more than moms who choose not to suffer, to not be martyrs for their families. It hates them for the same reason it hates any women who choose empowerment over martyrdom: because empowered women who love and take care of themselves are dangerous. They challenge the norms that cater to the comfort of men at the expense of women, *on the backs of us*. Empowered, self-loving women who free themselves from drowning are able to look around at their circumstances and dare to ask for more: more participation from their spouses, more respect, more fulfillment of their physical, mental, and emotional needs. They enter the workplace and compete with men for opportunities. They recognize mistreatment in their relationships and decide to find better. They don't sacrifice themselves at the altar of everyone else's needs. And that, my friend, is dangerous.

I am convinced that the world hates few things more than moms who choose not to suffer, to not be martyrs for their families. It hates them for the same reason it hates any women who choose empowerment over martyrdom: because empowered women who love and take care of themselves are dangerous.

Let them judge. Let them criticize. They do it because they are afraid of you, afraid of the power you possess when you aren't suffocating under the weight of loneliness and familial duty. You build your village and watch your world expand. Allow yourself to be astonished by what you can do when you are fearless, free, fulfilled.

You'll realize just how right they were to fear you.

And as for my mom? Well, I'm delighted to say that she has embraced village life in her senior years. She and my dad moved into an active adult community where everyone in the neighborhood is over fifty-five. Although my mom doesn't have a child to take care of anymore, she is building a foundation of help and support with other couples in the community. The younger couples give rides to doctors' appointments to the older community members who don't feel safe driving anymore. They cook meals for friends who have lost their spouses, coming over daily to comfort and support them. The older couples share sage wisdom about the beauty, and the grief, of reaching the final years. The entire community is in tune with one another—making sure that every neighbor feels taken care of, loved, appreciated, and honored.

Although it was late coming, my mom finally has her village.

Isn't it time to find your own village, too?

Cultivate Your Truth Trench

- **You weren't meant to struggle this way.** The shift from communal child-rearing to radical individualism has put immense pressure on mothers to fulfill numerous roles without adequate support. The traditional village support system is largely absent, leaving silent struggles and invisible labor that mothers were never meant to endure on their own.
- **You're a mother, not a martyr.** Challenge societal expectations that glorify martyrdom in motherhood. Understand that empowered, self-loving mothers who prioritize their well-being are a threat to the status quo and may face judgment and criticism. But your worth and value mean far more than critiques.
- **Build your own village.** Take proactive steps to build your own support network or village, whether through hiring help, trading resources with friends and neighbors, or exploring unconventional living arrangements.
- **Show them they were right to fear you.** There are certain people who fear empowered mothers who refuse to slowly suffocate under their maternal obligations. They despise the thought of what women can do when they are not buried under piles of dishes and laundry. They're right to fear you because you are powerful. *Show them.*

Chapter Fifteen

LGBTQ-ish

I spent most of my formative years longing for a village I didn't know existed or, at least, that I didn't think I was allowed to be a part of. I grew up in a proud, conservative Christian town and a proud, conservative Christian church. Towns and churches like that have a way of making people like me feel lonely.

I understood that something was different about me when my friends and I began noticing boys. We huddled together in the cafeteria, giggling over which boys were the cutest, which ones were the smartest or the funniest. We wondered out loud what our first kiss would feel like and which boy would be the one to deliver it.

And I wondered (not out loud) why none of them seemed to be noticing girls, too.

I learned very early about homosexuality. Towns like that, with churches like those, like to start that training young. I knew I wasn't supposed to be gay. I was pretty sure I *wasn't* gay because I definitely liked boys just like my friends did. I just didn't understand why it felt like I liked girls, too.

No one bothered to teach me the word *bisexual.* Since I didn't have a word for what I was—for people like me—I concluded that something was just wrong with me. So, I started the busy process of gaslighting myself about the part of me that liked girls. I decided that my eyes lingered on girls because I envied them. I wanted their perfect skin and straight teeth instead of my acne and braces. I wanted their curvy bodies instead of my boyish one. I told myself that the strong feelings I developed toward some of them weren't *crushes* like we had for the boys, even though I couldn't really place what those feelings were instead. The intense possessiveness I felt over a friend here and there didn't mean I liked her *like that.* I just had a weird way of making friendships. Too strong. Too attached.

I told myself that I was a strange and jealous person because those were the only labels I had to explain what made me different.

I told myself that I was a strange and jealous person because those were the only labels I had to explain what made me different.

It wasn't until college that I finally learned that there were lots of women like me. I wasn't weird after all! I was just kept separate, aloof, from a community that I had always belonged to. That I was born into. It took some pretty intense work to unravel the gaslighting I had done to myself as a kid. I had a lot of internalized homophobia to work through, a lot of needless shame to deconstruct.

Years of telling yourself that you are a jealous, possessive, and weird person instead of just a girl who happens to like boys *and* girls can do that to you. So, I had to do the difficult self-care of choosing to embrace who I was, who I am. I didn't deserve to beat myself up anymore.

I began telling my friends first—the ones who had known me the longest and who I was pretty sure were going to call me a knucklehead for not telling them sooner. I decided I'd also have to lead with this information when I began dating, *especially* when dating men, since some men, I learned, had very warped ideas about what dating a bisexual woman would mean for them. (Yes, I am monogamous; no, I'm not interested in threesomes.) Telling Charlie at the beginning of our relationship was a tad frightening only because I knew he shared my evangelical upbringing. I worried there might be some unconscious prejudice there despite his progressive leanings. I was wrong, and what I worried might be a deal-breaker for him ended up being something that he embraced with loving curiosity—a desire for me to reveal all of myself to him, even the hidden things. Through these conversations, I learned what a splendid and delicious gift it is to reveal my true self to others and be accepted for who I am, not for who I pretended to be.

Eventually, well into my thirties, I came out as bisexual to over half a million people on the internet. By then, I was married to Charlie, living a monogamous, heteronormative life, but it was important to me that women like me saw that women like them exist, so out I came.

The only problem was that I still hadn't come out to my parents. I guess, for a while at least, I just hoped that maybe they, and anyone who knew them, would never download TikTok. It wasn't until my separation from Charlie that I decided to share with them about my sexuality.

They did their best to take the news in stride, but as proud conservative Christians, this was a lot to process. We had many hard conversations during that time. A few that almost destroyed our relationship. I knew that nothing would make them stop loving me, but if they couldn't love *all* of me, I didn't know how we could move forward. I watched them struggle, too, trying to balance the religious teachings and convictions they held deeply with their overwhelming love of their only daughter.

A few months later, one of our family members came out as trans. My parents had a hard time digesting the news, but I noticed that, this time, they seemed a bit more compassionate. A bit more understanding. With time, with lots of discomfort and hard conversations, I watched them become more receptive to what it means to be queer. They asked questions and listened to the answers with open minds this time.

It's hard to say what made them finally try to understand. My best guess is that having someone in our family come out as trans in her fifties forced them to finally challenge their long-held belief that queerness is a choice. They understood that this family member would likely never "pass" as female by transitioning at this age. They recognized that she was likely in for a long road of criticism. Judgment. *Hate.* No one would choose to endure all of that if they didn't have to.

They realized for the first time that sexuality and gender identity may not be a choice after all. Maybe, just maybe, queer folks are born that way. And if they are born that way, then maybe all the things my parents had been taught about "the gay lifestyle" needed to be reconsidered. Finally, they understood. Their skepticism was replaced with compassion and acceptance. They embraced her the way she truly deserved.

And this newfound understanding made them finally understand me, too.

I had been out of the closet, living as my authentic self for years before my parents accepted me for who I am. I had come to understand that their disapproval of my identity said something about them, not about me. I had chosen to be patient, to love them and myself enough to keep trying to educate them, to coax them out of their long-held beliefs. Self-care was an act of hope—believing that my parents would one day understand and doing my best to help them get there.

I know that not everyone has the mental or emotional capacity to be patient with their families in this way. For some people, cutting unsupportive family out of their lives is the only way forward. It's just not worth the mental and emotional anguish to keep begging their parents to understand, to pivot, to release their rigid beliefs. So, for the queer folks here whose self-care took (or will take) the form of cutting off unsupportive family members, just know that you are valid. You made the right choice. And you are very brave.

Choosing to live as your true, authentic self is the greatest act of self-care a person can do for themselves. *Coming out* is a term that's owned by the LGBTQ community. It is a process that must be taken very seriously because coming out can put a person's mental, emotional, and even physical safety at risk. Most of us will never have to come out in a way that puts us in danger, but almost all of us will, at some point, have to "come out" in our own way. We will have to choose between being our authentic selves or hiding parts of ourselves away from the world.

Choosing to live as your true, authentic self is the greatest act of self-care a person can do for themselves.

Being authentic, being real, is scary and sometimes comes with consequences. If we are honest with ourselves, we all have bits of who we are that we have hidden from the world to avoid shame or criticism. We all have parts of ourselves that we would love to share with the people we care about, but our fear of rejection or disapproval keeps us quiet.

Some people have different spiritual or political beliefs than their friends and family and are afraid that opening up about them will cause a rift. Some have interests they fear other people will call weird, cringy, or stupid. We fear rejection, so we choose to hide instead, to keep a part of who we are in the shadows. We let them love a fraction of us. We miss out on being loved in our completeness.

We fear rejection, so we choose to hide instead, to keep a part of who we are in the shadows. We let them love a fraction of us. We miss out on being loved in our completeness.

As women and as humans, we can't care about ourselves and expect others to care about us in a way that feels fulfilling unless we share who our essential self really is. To the extent that it is safe for us to do so, it is time to reveal our full, immaculate, mesmerizing selves. When possible, we can help people understand us better and learn to accept us for who we are. When impossible, we can love ourselves enough to walk away without chasing or convincing. We will never beg for acceptance. We will simply be and be well.

Coming out as bisexual to the world and to my family was the first step toward embracing this kind of radical self-acceptance and self-expression. I am learning slowly, purposefully, how to reveal my true self to the world without fear of what people will think. It's a process. It's hard to release the deeply entrenched desire to be pleasing to other people, and I'm no exception. But as I learn how to unapologetically reveal my true self to the world—my beliefs, my opinions, even my shortcomings—I'm discovering a mesmerizing truth:

When you are your authentic self, you will find your people.

Yes, there will be people who abandon you when you reveal your true self. That part will always sting. But for every person who exits your life, there will be many, many more who enter it. You will find that there are people who understand, who relate, who need to hear your story to finally accept their own. Free to reveal who you truly are, without shame or remorse, you will find community with people who can finally be free, too. As I've shared about my bisexuality, my marriage separation, my challenges (and mistakes) in parenting my kids, and my grappling with my faith, I've alienated people for sure. But, friend, *when I tell you* how many more people have taken their place! I have found real community and friendship. I've found support in ways I've truly never known and *so many people* who intimately understand me.

When you are your authentic self, you will find your people.

I am finally free, and my friend, you deserve to be free, too. Like my therapist said so many years ago, "Sometimes the cages we find ourselves in are of our own making. If we would only push the door open, if we would take that first step out of the 'safety' (and danger) of the cage, we would find freedom is ours for the taking: freedom to be ourselves, to love ourselves, to express every part of our souls to the world, and to find *our people.*" You deserve that freedom, and so do I.

We are done hiding in closets and cages.

Cultivate Your Truth Trench

- **You deserve to be loved in your completeness.** The people who belong at your table are the ones who are able to love you for *all* of who you are. You deserve to reveal yourself fully to the people who claim to love you. Acceptance may take time and require difficult conversations. Love yourself enough to walk away from anyone, including family, who won't love you in your fullness.
- **Living authentically allows you to be loved authentically.** Embrace the importance of authenticity and self-expression, even in the face of societal pressures or familial expectations. Choosing authenticity is an act of self-care and liberation, allowing you to live fully as you are and to be loved fully, too.
- **Self-care inspires connection and community.** When you do the difficult work of self-care, you build self-respect. Self-respect compels you to find and embrace people who love you for who you are. As you do this work, you will attract like-minded people and build a supportive community.
- **No more closets and cages.** You were not designed to live in imprisonment and solitude. Taking brave steps toward your authentic self leads to the freedom to be who you are and to be embraced as your truest self.

Chapter Sixteen

Clinking Dishes

My only memories of my extended family are from brief childhood visits to Jacksonville, Florida, where the entire family lived.

I remember fondly the smell of bacon and the sound of clinking dishes coming from my aunt's kitchen every morning in those days. The way my aunt embraced me warmly, the smell of her shampoo. How my uncle would brightly exclaim, "Hello, little Amber!" from his perch at the kitchen table.

I loved my extended family. They were so funny and carefree—so unlike my parents who, in my youth, *felt* very strict. I liked the laughter I always heard around my aunts, uncles, cousins, and grandparents—the loud voices, the impassioned conversations, the joy they all seemed to share that you tend to only see in children. They were so much fun, until they weren't.

What I know now, which I didn't know then, was that most of my family members—basically everyone except my beloved aunt—were fun because they were drunk. *Always* drunk. When I was six years old, my parents made the hard decision to separate me from them for good. My family members weren't bad people. In fact, they were very good people. But bad habits bring bad health, bad decisions, and sometimes irreversible damage. My parents didn't want me growing up glamorizing alcohol. They didn't want me to think *normal* meant cracking open a Bud Light with breakfast. Since my family wouldn't change, couldn't choose us over alcohol, my parents chose me over them.

I didn't understand the depth of their sacrifice until I became a mom myself. Having children of my own showed me everything that my parents, particularly my mom, gave up in exchange for breaking the cycle. My mom lost her village. However imperfect, and however far away they were, they were still her family. They never hurt her or me, and despite their battle with addiction, they were *her people*—people she could have turned to when times were tough had she not cut them out of our lives.

My parents endured scorn from the family members they left behind who didn't understand what the big deal was. They called my parents snooty, conceited, full of themselves. I'm sure that hurt my parents. I'm also sure they might have questioned their decision from time to time, too. It's so easy to gaslight ourselves about the choices we make, especially when our families are concerned. But my parents trusted themselves anyway and stuck to what they felt was best for me and my future. They had the courage to tell their parents and siblings that they'd got it wrong—not that they were bad people, not that they didn't deserve love, but that they had made choices that my parents didn't want their daughter to make. My parents were willing to stand in the gap that would protect me from becoming like them.

I'll always miss the sound of clinking dishes and sizzling bacon in my aunt's house on those summer visits, the intimacy of waking up to a house filled with people who share my blood. I'll always feel a little envious of my friends who experienced the incomparable love of a big family. That said, I will never regret my parents' decision to break the cycle of alcoholism to give me a chance at a different life.

There is no form of badassery quite like cycle breaking. *Cycle breaking* is a term that I hadn't heard of until it became popular on TikTok and Instagram. The term is new, but the idea is very old. Being a cycle breaker means recognizing unhealthy cycles of behavior within our families and making choices to break those cycles. Many things about our traits, attitudes, beliefs, and values are influenced not just by our parents but also by generations of family members before us. These things are reinforced and passed along from generation to generation. Cycle breakers are people who decide to be the first generation to stop the spread of unhealthy patterns in their family. Just as a flame can't spread across a row of matches if one match is pulled away from the line, unhealthy behaviors can't pass through families if one generation steps back and makes a change. My parents were the first cycle breakers in my family. Because of their sacrifice, I get to be a cycle breaker, too.

Being a cycle breaker means recognizing unhealthy cycles of behavior within our families and making choices to break those cycles.

These are the moments in life that distinguish true self-care, the kind of self-care that can actually nourish and sustain, from potato chip self-care. Empty calorie, potato chip self-care says *don't ruffle feathers, don't make waves. Just do what you have to do to keep the family happy*. Potato chip self-care tells us to do the easy thing because easy things feel better. Potato chips put a Band-Aid on a problem. They ease our hunger for a moment, but they cannot fix the problem. Those empty calories can't make us feel full, and even if they make us feel better at first, once they're back in the pantry, we usually feel worse afterward.

Real self-care tells us that sometimes the right thing doesn't feel great. Nourishing self-care sometimes means enduring a temporary discomfort in exchange for long-term peace and happiness. Looking back at my childhood now that I am an adult, I think this might have been one of the most important lessons my parents taught me.

Real self-care tells us that sometimes the right thing doesn't feel great. Nourishing self-care sometimes means enduring a temporary discomfort in exchange for long-term peace and happiness.

Because of them, I get to be a cycle breaker with my kids. Thankfully, I don't have to break the cycle of alcoholism because my parents broke that one already. But there are cycles that still need to be broken. Unlike my parents, who had to walk away from family to break cycles, I am trying to break cycles while my parents are watching.

This has added a layer of difficulty to my cycle-breaking journey. Telling my parents that I think they got some things wrong isn't easy. It's not something that I enjoy communicating to them, and it's probably not something they love to hear. But we are family. We love one another, and we are willing to have important conversations that don't feel good.

I don't love discussing these things publicly because I feel like I'm betraying my parents. Nonetheless, I think there is usefulness in sharing a couple examples of how I am breaking cycles for my kids because maybe you are doing the same and don't know where to start. You may also need to see a positive example of someone breaking these cycles with their families in a way that is respectful and focused on keeping the family together.

Before I continue, just understand that it is okay to disagree with some of the choices your parents made. It doesn't mean you had bad parents. It may mean simply that the world has changed since they were new parents. We have new information now, and when you know better, you do better.

One of the cycles I am breaking is the way I talk about mental health with my kids. Growing up, I felt like mental health was a taboo subject. My mom had diagnosed depression. My dad, I'm pretty sure, had undiagnosed anxiety. Both of my parents seemed to have a complicated relationship with their mental health. They went through seasons of going to therapy, taking medications that would help, and being intentional about taking good care of themselves. Other times, their mental health seemed to not be a priority at all. During those times, our house became pretty dysfunctional. Without knowing it, my parents passed along to me a very passive view of my mental health that it is something to be taken care of when you can, but that is ultimately out of your control. Charlie and I are breaking cycles by being an example of stability with our kids when it comes to our mental health. We normalize going to therapy and taking our prescribed medications. We sometimes have to take accountability for when our mental health is not in check, choosing to apologize to our kids and then do the work to fix it. We started teaching them emotion words at an early age, giving them the language to communicate and understand their feelings. The self-care of our mental health isn't done quietly or in secret. In our home, we take care of our mental health loudly.

The self-care of our mental health isn't done quietly or in secret. In our home, we take care of our mental health loudly.

We are also breaking cycles of faith and religious trauma, which has been particularly uncomfortable for us. Charlie and I are very wounded by the present-day church. We feel that too many Christian people have lost sight of Christ and embraced instead a very white-washed Christian nationalism that is cruel and dangerous—devoid of the love of Jesus. They are so busy judging people for whom they love, how they identify, swearing, or dressing "immodestly" that they have forgotten how to judge the quality and nature of their own hearts.

We don't want our children embracing these values. We don't go to church, and we're not sure if we will go back. We read our Bibles and practice our faith at home. We will keep doing so until the church becomes a place of love and acceptance that Christ meant it to be. We are teaching our children about God but giving them freedom to question what we believe. Christianity was imparted to me by my parents as though it was an inheritance. I was just as Christian as I was white, female, and blue-eyed. I don't recall being encouraged to explore my own beliefs, interrogate them, and see if I truly believed. My kids will get to do that. My parents strongly disagree with this approach to faith, and that hurts for us all. But it is our nonnegotiable decision to break the chains of religion and give our kids the freedom to believe what feels right to them.

Being cycle breakers in our family has meant setting boundaries, expressing our desire for our children's upbringing, having tough conversations, and insisting that our wishes are respected. This is the hard and rewarding work of real self-care. There is no bubble bath or rejuvenating face mask that can bring the peace and prolonged happiness of

Being cycle breakers in our family has meant setting boundaries, expressing our desire for our children's upbringing, having tough conversations, and insisting that our wishes are respected.

being authentic with ourselves and our families. It is bad ass to take good care of yourself. It is *a badass move* to choose the uncomfortable work of cycle breaking.

When we do this work, we not only break cycles for children. We break them for our peers—our friends looking on, who watch us step out of dysfunctional cycles and realize that they can do the same. We break cycles for our little siblings, our nieces and nephews, our cousins, and all the little girls coming up behind us.

We break the cycles so that they don't have to.

We break the cycles so that they don't have to.

As we break harmful cycles in our families, we create new ones that are healthy. We embrace the happy parts of our families—the traditions, the joy. If there are no happy memories to hold on to, we make our own. We create a cycle of health and well-being for the generations to come.

These days, I still get to hear clinking dishes and sizzling bacon in the morning. Only now, I'm the one in the kitchen, lovingly making breakfast for my family. Sober. Clear minded. Healthy. I am creating memories for my kids that are like the ones from those days in my aunt's kitchen, but theirs won't be tainted by addiction. I am giving my children the moments I always wished I could have when I was their age.

Self-care for me and for my children is being willing to abolish unhealthy cycles and establish healthy routines in their place.

Cultivate Your Truth Trench

- **Breaking cycles is an act of self-care (and badassery).** Embrace the idea of being a cycle-breaker in your family. This means bravely stepping up to dismantle negative patterns and create a healthier environment for yourself and future generations.
- **Boundaries are badass, too.** Learn to set boundaries that protect your values and well-being within your family dynamic. It's okay to assert your needs and desires, even if it causes temporary discomfort. And if you are raising children of your own, they deserve to see an example of how it's done.
- **Breaking cycles branches outward.** Your actions as a cycle breaker inspire positive change not only in your own family but also in your wider community. Lead by example and show others that breaking free from harmful patterns is possible.
- **Out with the old, in with the new.** Take joy in creating new family traditions and memories that are free from negativity or dysfunction. Build a legacy of love, joy, and togetherness for future generations to cherish. You have the power to shape a bright future for yourself and those you love.

Chapter Seventeen

Thermostat

Charlie once told me that I am the thermostat for the household. He said I set the emotional temperature for everyone in the family.

It was an odd thing to hear. In what world does it make sense for people to take their emotional cues from me? I am basically the Michael Scott of emotional range. Much like the gregarious and often emotionally dysregulated lead character from *The Office*, my emotional intensity ping-pongs back and forth from zero to ten and zips right past the gentler numbers in the middle. Am I *really* the person we want in charge of setting the emotional temperature of the house?

Why in God's name am I expected to be responsible for everyone else's mood? That seems like too much to expect from one person. I hold a lot of resentment around the idea that I should have to constantly regulate my own emotional temperature for the comfort of everyone else in my home. I especially resent the idea that if *other people* in the house are dysregulated, then it's because the thermostat isn't functioning properly—*I* am not functioning properly.

What do I do with that? Am I supposed to be, as Charlie said, the family's thermostat?

I decided that he was half right, half wrong. I could accept the parts of this idea that were right while setting boundaries around the ones that were wrong. Self-care would look like accepting an inconvenient truth that would benefit my family (that I am responsible for regulating my emotions for the sake of my kids) while rejecting unfair expectations that would make my life harder (that I am responsible for *everyone else's* emotions).

The first thing I decided is that I am not responsible for the feelings and emotional temperature of other adults, including my husband. I firmly believe that I am not accountable for the feelings of grown-ups, even if they happen to be my spouse. It's liberating. And while I care deeply for my husband and want to make his emotional world as comfortable as possible, I also recognize that his emotional well-being is his own responsibility. This is a boundary I set with him, and after laying out why I felt it was unfair to put the burden of his feelings on me, he completely agreed.

The second thing I decided was that I *am* responsible for the emotional temperature of my kids. They are little and don't have good coping skills yet. My emotions can have a big impact on them. When I am upset, when I am anxious, when I am frustrated, my children experience those feelings right along with me as though they are feeling them, too. It is reasonable, then, that I regulate my big (and small) emotions around them.

For me, self-care in this matter has looked like accepting a truth that I don't like very much. And yes, I will die on this hill: If we love ourselves and our families, sometimes true self-care—the kind that can genuinely fulfill—means thinking of what is best for our entire family unit. It's like my favorite quote from the movie *A Beautiful Mind:* "The best for the group comes when everyone in the group does what's best for himself and the group." Most of what we see in trendy self-care culture is highly individualistic and self-focused, and for the most part, I think that's great. But as parents, there can be no "best" for ourselves that doesn't include the best for our children. My best is inextricably linked to their best.

But as parents, there can be no "best" for ourselves that doesn't include the best for our children. My best is inextricably linked to their best.

I choose to see Charlie and myself more like those water safety flags at the beach than as a thermostat. We are not a thermostat. We do not *control* the emotions of the people in our house. Instead, we are a signal. Just as locals and vacationers look to the water safety flags to know whether there is safety or danger in the water, our kids do the same with us. To them, we are the *indicator* of what the conditions in the house are going to be. We don't control their emotions, but we do impact them by the way we choose to regulate (or dysregulate) our own. I want our kids to feel safe, comfortable, and at ease in our home. They are at their best that way, and in turn, Charlie and I can be at our best.

What that means for my personal journey of practicing self-care with my family is to recognize two simultaneous truths. The first is that my emotions have an impact on my children and need to be expressed responsibly. The second is that I do not have to hide my emotions from my children. In fact, hiding my very human feelings does a disservice to us all. Instead of hiding my feelings, I can be honest about how I feel, while establishing safety and comfort for my kids.

Instead of hiding my feelings, I can be honest about how I feel, while establishing safety and comfort for my kids.

It's been a hard process, but I'm getting there. I'm learning how resilient my kids are. I used to think that talking to them about what I was feeling was a no-no. We're not supposed to make our kids feel responsible for our burdens, right? I think that's something a lot of us were taught about parenthood. I'm learning, though, that my kids are actually very capable of understanding my emotions when I communicate them. It's a lot easier for my kids when I say, "I'm sorry, kiddos, mommy is really sad right now," than when I try to white-knuckle my way through my feelings and leave my kids wondering if they did something wrong.

I can show my children that I am a human, a human who feels, a human who is responsible for her own feelings. I can show them that we can decide for ourselves whose emotions we are willing to be responsible for: in my case, never for adults, but always for my children—at least until they get older and can be responsible for their own. Self-care is deciding what I am responsible for and what I am not and drawing boundaries between the two.

Cultivate Your Truth Trench

- **You don't set the temperature.** While you grapple with the concept of being the emotional thermostat for your family, remember that it doesn't all have to be on your shoulders. Yes, you're accountable for your kids' emotional well-being, but you *cannot* and *should not* bear the burden of regulating other adults' emotions.
- **Establish boundaries about what is reasonable and what isn't.** It is reasonable for you to be responsible for the feelings of your children since they look to you for cues about the emotional climate of the household and your actions set the tone. If grown-ups, including your spouse, expect you to do the same for them, you may need to have hard conversations and set firm boundaries.
- **Your kids deserve a mother who feels.** It doesn't do you or your children any good for you to pretend you do not feel things. Showing your emotions to your children, when done consciously and carefully, teaches them valuable tools like compassion and empathy. They are able to hone those skills with you in a safe environment.
- **Your self-regulation creates safety for your children's emotions.** By communicating that they're not responsible for your feelings, you empower your children to navigate their emotional world while maintaining a sense of security. It's a valuable lesson in emotional literacy and personal boundaries.

Chapter Eighteen
The Unaesthetic Aesthetic

The most delicious irony of sitting down to write this chapter about aesthetic homemaking is that I just shoved a pile of clean laundry off my bed to clear a spot for me to work.

I have resigned myself to the fact that my home's aesthetic will never be Instagram worthy. I will never have flawlessly synchronized colors in each room. I bought our furniture on Amazon, and most of my walls are bare. My children inherited my inability to close kitchen cabinets or put lids back on drinks and sauce bottles. Charlie passed down his propensity to horde things that are basically obsolete because *what if he needs them one day and doesn't have them*? (for example, he has ninety-six gallon-size bags filled to the top with wires for phones and computers he doesn't even have anymore).

I used to really struggle with comparing myself to the aesthetic wives and moms out there. I wondered how they seemed to have it all together. Perfect marriages, perfect kids. Perfect hair, never out of place. Perfect lives. To be honest, I still struggle with it, even now that the illusion of their "perfect" lives has been shattered. We all know that those millennial beige, Rae Dun–outfitted, meticulously appointed aesthetic homes and Instagram feeds aren't real life. They are a carefully curated collection of highlight reels, chosen because they fit an image of perfection that attracts praise and attention. It's not a bad thing. It's just . . . not real.

Why do I try to make my *entire life* reflect the perfection that those women show from only *snippets* of theirs? Why do I feel like a failure when I can't make my life look like the mirage I see on social media?

Why do I try to make my *entire life* reflect the perfection that those women show from only *snippets* of theirs? Why do I feel like a failure when I can't make my life look like the mirage I see on social media?

It's natural to compare ourselves to other people. But it's also torturous. It's much worse when we compare ourselves to other women because it makes us ask a question that nobody really wants the answer to: *What does she have that I don't have?* And because we struggle with insecurities and we see ourselves as somehow less competent and capable than other women, we arrive at the wrong conclusions. We launch ourselves into a psychological spin cycle that only does more damage to our self-esteem.

Toxic, consumeristic self-care culture tells us that taking good care of ourselves means having a perfectly clean and organized household. I tend to get lost down TikTok scroll holes watching "restocking videos." Elegant women buy things that come in containers, then remove the things from those containers and put them in new containers. Then, they throw the original containers in the trash. They print new labels from their Dymo printers, made in pretty, uniform script to tell them what's in the container (since they threw away the container that already had a label on it). They put these newly labeled, uniform containers in their perfectly organized pantry, fully stocked with identical clear bins and trays. Not a cardboard cereal box in sight.

It looks stylish and functional and expensive. Like, so expensive that I cannot comprehend how they afford it all. But when I check their caption, I see how they afford it: *#ad. #paidpartnership. #linkinbio. Use code MELISSA20 at checkout!* Listen, I'm not here to put down women for using their platforms to make money. I am all for women empowering ourselves to be financially independent or simply financially more comfortable. I just sometimes wish that the brands who pay for these influencer ads—who tell these influencers exactly how to pitch and sell the product—thought about the message they are sending to women. It's a message of excess. Capitalism. Privilege. "Self-care" looks like buying things that come in containers, just to buy different containers to put them in because they're *aesthetic*. The subtle message is that "self-care" is taking two hours to put the grocery shopping away because everything has to be "just so."

That image of wealth and luxury is just not realistic or accessible to everyone, but the impulse to compare ourselves to women like that certainly is. We stack ourselves up against these images of perfection and declare ourselves less than.

That image of wealth and luxury is just not realistic or accessible to everyone, but the impulse to compare ourselves to women like that certainly is. We stack ourselves up against these images of perfection and declare ourselves less than.

My journey has meant redefining my idea of success when it comes to my home. I am not willing or able to make it aesthetic, so why make aesthetic the goal? Keeping a house successfully can mean many things, and it's up to me to decide what success looks like. I've decided that for me, success is having a home that makes sense for my specific needs. It means that the house works for me, not the other way around. This is not an original idea; I first heard this concept from K. C. Davis, who authored the book *How to Keep House While Drowning.* The basic idea is that my house should be structured in a way that makes life easier for me. Rather than me existing to serve my house, my house exists to serve me.

What I like about this concept is that it leaves room for individual differences in the way we all keep house. If women who keep those aesthetic homes find joy in that labor, if it makes their home more comfortable and peaceful to live in, then their house is existing to serve them. I do not find comfort or joy *at all* in that kind of labor. If I force myself to follow these aesthetic trends that I do not enjoy, I am serving my home. It is not serving me.

When it comes to how I keep my home, self-care has meant deciding what it means for the home to be serving me and using *that* as my metric for success. As long as my home is serving me rather than the other way around, then I am succeeding at homemaking.

When it comes to how I keep my home, self-care has meant deciding what it means for the home to be serving me and using *that* as my metric for success. As long as my home is serving me rather than the other way around, then I am succeeding at homemaking.

My first step toward making my home work for me was to get rid of my goddamn place mats and fabric napkins. Do you know what an absolute pain those things have been to me? Every evening, after dinner, I clean away the dirty plates and utensils and spread in their place my useless table décor. Because, let's be honest, that's what it was. We didn't use the place mats and napkins. They were *show napkins*. So, each morning, when the kids had breakfast, I swept away the place mats and napkins, stored them in the pantry, and put in their place the cheap plastic plates and toss-away napkins that we actually ate with. When the kids left for school, I picked up the dirty dishes, retrieved all the decorative crap from the pantry, and put it back on the table. And this I did three times a day, every day. Who in the hell was I trying to impress? No one saw this house most days except me. So, I got rid of them. My kitchen table stays bare 24/7, except for at mealtimes when the real dishes are out. I have saved so much time and aggravation with this tiny change in routine, and that is what truly brings me joy.

Next, I moved everyone's clothes into one closet. I know that when the kids are older, they will want their own closets (and will be responsible for their own laundry), but as long as they're little and still relying on me to take care of their clothes, I'm keeping it all in one convenient place. Does my closet look completely overrun and disorganized most days? Yes. But does it make my laundry routine *so much freaking easier?* Also yes. When laundry is done, I pile it all into a laundry basket and take it straight to our family closet. I'm able to fold, hang, and put away everyone's clothing all at once without making trips all around the house.

I bought hanging baskets and adhered them to the mirrors in our bathroom. They're technically shower caddies, not aesthetically pleasing at all. But I store in them all the things that Charlie and I tend to grab for in the bathroom—soap, toothpaste, face cleanser, moisturizers, the works. Now, it's super easy for us to get to our things, and we have the added benefit of an empty bathroom countertop. This has made it *so much easier* to keep the surfaces clean. Rather than having to move all our crap off the counter before I can clean, I just pull out the cleaning spray and get to work. Charlie and I are both very fixated on having a clean bathroom, and we both get irritable when it's a mess. This small change to our routine, though it wouldn't look great in an Instagram photo, brings joy and peace of mind.

This small change to our routine, though it wouldn't look great in an Instagram photo, brings joy and peace of mind.

Wherever possible, I have chosen function over aesthetic. I don't like keeping curtains clean and pressed, so I didn't hang any. I hate having to dust artsy decorative pieces on my surfaces, so I got rid of them. I don't mind eating my Frosted Flakes out of the box they came in, so that's how they stay in my pantry. I call it my unaesthetic aesthetic, and it's working out great! I don't feel the need to compare myself to other women whose homes are more beautiful or Pinterest-worthy than mine because I have a different standard than those women. My home is a success because it serves me and my unique needs. It makes my life easier, not harder.

I think the beautiful thing about choosing real self-care is that it gives us room to be exactly who we are, to create the kind of world in which we want to live.

I think the beautiful thing about choosing real self-care is that it gives us room to be exactly who we are, to create the kind of world in which we want to live. It's liberating to reject the consumeristic idea of self-care that only focuses on superficial aesthetics and luxury. We have the power to choose whatever form of self-care works best for us, whether it's the traditional or the unconventional way. The kind of self-care that truly fulfills us is the kind that asks what we need to be happy and whole and then relentlessly pursues those things. Nourishing self-care is all about authenticity; it doesn't compare or judge us for being different or doing things our own way.

In this moment, I will choose to live authentically and leave my pile of clean clothes on the floor until tomorrow. This is my house. It serves me. I do not serve it.

That is meaningful self-care.

Cultivate Your Truth Trench

- **You deserve a home that serves your needs.** Instead of striving for an Instagram-worthy aesthetic, redefine success based on what works for you and your family's specific needs. Your home should serve you, not the other way around.
- **What someone else calls self-care might feel like labor to you.** Some people find joy and fulfillment in creating aesthetic homes. They do it because it fills their tank. If those tasks feel like they drain yours—if they feel like labor instead of self-care—you don't need to bother with them. Self-care, when it comes to homemaking, often means daring to do what brings ease in a culture that wants women to exhaust themselves.
- **Self-care prioritizes function over aesthetic (if that's what matters to you).** Opt for practical solutions that make your life easier, even if they don't fit conventional aesthetic standards. Focus on what brings you joy and peace of mind rather than chasing trends.
- **Your home is a sacred place of self-expression.** Celebrate your individuality and create a home environment that reflects who you are, regardless of societal expectations. Your home is a success when it aligns with your values and makes daily life more manageable.

Chapter Nineteen
Sandwiched

I am sitting down to write this chapter just one week after a member of my extended family dropped dead with no warning. His name was Mitchell. One minute, Mitchell was standing up from his chair to flip the burgers on the grill; the next he was face down on the concrete, dead. They said it was a pulmonary embolism. He was probably deceased before he hit the ground.

If I seem emotionally disconnected from this, it's because I am. I didn't know him. In fact, I never even met him. He was family but twice removed. My dad was married before he married my mom, and he and his first wife had my half-sister, Cristi. My dad later married my mom, and they had me. My dad's first wife went on to marry Mitchell, who became my half-sister's stepdad. Although I never got to know Mitchell, I of course know my half-sister, Cristi. It is through the lens of her "new normal" in the aftermath of her stepdad's passing that I write this chapter.

My sister is in her early fifties. She has two sons, my nephews, both just barely out of high school. She is divorced, has been since the children were babies. She devoted her peak adult years to raising her boys alone (she had the kind of custody agreement that was typical in the early 2000s, where dad only had the kids every other weekend). Her boys are now beginning to gain their independence, both testing their wings for the first time on their own. But of course, being as young as they are, my sister is still very involved in their lives.

She is young and active, vivacious and full of life. Having completed her obligations to her young children, she is now in a place to more fully explore her own dreams: finding a career that fulfills rather than one that just pays the bills, making friends, getting more involved in hobbies, maybe hitting the dating scene again? She deserves it. Life gave her a lot of lemons, and she is finally in the lemonade years.

But now, just as her new life is on the horizon, she is about to find herself in the role, once again, of caretaker. Her mom, Sybil, is a lovely woman, full of life and energy. Mitchell provided a wonderful life for her, and I'm sure he made arrangements for taking care of her financially following his death. However, being taken care of financially does not soothe the anguish of a spouse departed too soon, a husband plucked up before his time. She is suddenly alone in a house that probably feels far too big for one person. Suddenly, she is a widow.

I can't help but find my thoughts turning toward my sister in this moment. Her life changed just as suddenly and just as profoundly as Sybil's did the day that Mitchell died. She is now going to be responsible for easing her mom through the long and difficult journey of grief and healing. She will be her mother's emotional support system for what I imagine will be years. When her mother gets a bit older and less independent, it will be my sister's job to take care of her mental and physical needs, too.

So, she finds herself sandwiched. Sandwiched between almost-grown kids who still need her guidance and support and a now-widowed mother who will begin leaning more and more heavily on her as the years go on. Although I believe my sister is doing her best to have a positive attitude about this new normal, I know it can't be easy.

A lot of us, particularly millennials like me, are headed for the sandwichy time of our lives. The time when we are sandwiched between caring for children who still require financial, emotional, and physical support and aging parents who become increasingly dependent on us as they age. Learning of Mitchell's unexpected death threw into stark relief for me the reality that this will be in my future—grieving the loss of one parent and caring for the other while trying to keep my kids, my marriage, my career, and my household afloat—and I'm not sure I'm ready for that responsibility.

It's a responsibility that, despite having a husband who is willing and able to help me and provide support when he can, will *always* default to me. As women, we are expected to be the caretakers of our families, and as we discussed before, we are expected to do it in the absence of a village. We feel the weight of expectations of everyone around us, expecting us to take care of everyone's needs while somehow finding time to take care of our own. And if we can't? Well, how selfish of us. How dare we fail to meet our familial obligations? How *dare* we suggest that we're being stretched too thin?

While preparing to write this chapter, I did a quick Google search to see what useful info is out there about self-care for the sandwiched generation. What I found was disappointing at best, negligent at worst. I found loads of well-meaning listicles outlining "Five Fabulous Self-Care Tips for the Sandwiched Generation," which provided such helpful tidbits as *get more sleep, maintain a healthy diet, make time to laugh,* and *aim for regular exercise.*

Umm. Excuse the absolute hell out of me?

Listen, I am a thirty-something millennial with two young kids. I am healthy, my kids are healthy, my husband is healthy. We live comfortably within our means and without much worry over finances. We have my parents nearby to help. And I *still* struggle to do all of those things. Get more sleep, you say? Okay, great. You want to watch my kids while I do that? Make time to laugh? What does that even mean? How do I *make time* to laugh?

This is my issue with the useless, feckless "self-care" gurus that are out there today. They provide tips for taking care of yourself in hard times without ever telling you *how* to accomplish those things. They issue performative instructions that have the veneer of helpfulness but provide no real value.

This is my issue with the useless, feckless "self-care" gurus that are out there today. They provide tips for taking care of yourself in hard times without ever telling you *how* to accomplish those things. They issue performative instructions that have the veneer of helpfulness but provide no real value.

Self-care in the sandwiched years is not as simple as keeping a healthy diet or getting more sleep. It's about the hard work—hear me, the *hard work*—of setting limits with yourself and others about what you are willing to be responsible for and what you are not. It's about being willing to say no. No, even when it's inconvenient. No, even when it lets other people down.

I've had this conversation often with my friend who is living in the epitome of the sandwiched years. She has four children, two of them grown(ish) and two of them in elementary school. She lived, for many years, with both of her parents residing in her home. At the peak of the COVID outbreak, her mother became very ill and needed almost constant care. During that time, my friend also became ill with a mysterious condition that even the best California doctors couldn't identify. Then, suddenly, her husband lost his job. My friend found herself sick, caring for her ailing mother, taking care of her two young children, nurturing the growth and burgeoning adulthood of her older kids, tending to her father who was worried sick about his wife's health, and also clinging desperately to a job she really couldn't manage anymore.

She also had no sense of boundaries. This kind, dear woman would say yes to anyone who asked her. No matter how big or small the imposition, no matter how little time or energy she had available to give, my friend could never say no. Over time, my sparkling friend began to lose her sparkle. Her essence began to dull. She got sicker. Her mother passed away. Her job became more demanding and little by little, she began to disappear. It took almost yessing herself into the grave before she realized that she had to set limits around her yesses, before she learned that *no* is an act of self-compassion that only she could give herself.

It took almost yessing herself into the grave before she realized that she had to set limits around her yesses, before she learned that *no* is an act of self-compassion that only she could give herself.

I know that I will need to start preparing myself for my own sandwiched years soon. I had kids in my early thirties, which means I will likely still have young children at home when my parents begin the transition to needing me more and more. Since millennials, in general, waited until we were older to have kids, I bet a lot of you are in the same boat. It's not something I love thinking about. No one wants to think about their parents slowly losing their independence, marching on toward the end of their story. Nonetheless, it's important that we begin the good habits of self-care and boundary setting now so that we can easily apply them when it's our turn in the sandwich.

What are those good habits? I think one of the most important habits is actually a mindset. It is divorcing ourselves from the idea that we have to do it all on our own, that we are somehow weak or incapable if we ask for help. Accepting help and delegating responsibilities is not a weakness. It is a necessary step in managing the demands of being sandwiched between two generations who need us.

Accepting help and delegating responsibilities is not a weakness. It is a necessary step in managing the demands of being sandwiched between two generations who need us.

Another good habit, which we should be practicing in our daily lives anyway, is setting limits around what we are willing to say yes to. Self-care, in its proper place, means saying yes only when we truly mean it, when we have the authentic desire to help or to serve. Otherwise, we need to learn the difficult but compassionate art of saying no. No, when friends pressure us to hang out but we haven't got the energy. No, when the PTO says we need to volunteer time and we have none to give. No, when we'd honestly just rather lay in bed and binge Netflix. Why? Because our time, our energy, our mental and emotional health are limited, and it is our responsibility to guard them well.

Lastly, we need to accept that self-care isn't selfish, even when so many other people need our care, too. In fact, engaging in meaningful self-care is necessary if we are going to take care of others well. When we are overwhelmed and exhausted, having nothing to give, it is impossible to be patient, understanding, and effective caregivers to the people we love.

We care best for others when we care for ourselves.

My sister has a long road ahead of learning to walk the sandwiched years with grace. She will have her own grief to process. She will have to reconcile her complicated feelings about craving freedom while feeling a sense of duty to her aging mother. My hope for her, for you, for myself is that as we embark on the sandwiched years, we do it with self-love, self-respect, and copious amounts of self-compassion.

My hope for her, for you, for myself is that as we embark on the sandwiched years, we do it with self-love, self-respect, and copious amounts of self-compassion.

A life of meaningful self-care is about escaping cages, choosing to be free from self-made constraints that keep us tethered and unhappy.

We cannot let the sandwiched years become a cage of our own making.

Cultivate Your Truth Trench

- **You deserve self-care, even in the sandwich.** Self-care, in any season of life but especially in the sandwiched years, goes beyond simple tips like getting more sleep and eating well. It's about setting firm boundaries, learning to say no when necessary, and prioritizing your own well-being amid competing demands.
- **It is very brave to ask for help.** Shift your mindset away from feeling weak or incapable when asking for assistance. Accepting help and delegating responsibilities is crucial for managing demands of caring for multiple generations.
- **"No" is a full sentence that requires no explanation.** Practice saying no when you don't genuinely have the energy or desire to take on additional responsibilities. Protect your time, energy, and mental health by being selective about what you agree to.
- **We care best for others when we care for ourselves.** Engaging in meaningful self-care isn't selfish, even when others rely on you for care. Prioritizing your own well-being enables you to be a more patient, understanding, and effective caregiver to those you love.

Chapter Twenty
Bubble Baths

The exhaustion I feel as a mom can't just be washed away with a bubble bath, yet I am constantly told by men and women alike to just "go take a nice bath" when the stress of my kids, my marriage, and my career become absolutely too damn much.

I'm thankful that my kids are a bit older now. I can finally shower without a bassinet on the other side of the shower curtain. Now that the kids are in school, I have opportunities to do the things that are difficult to do when kids are around. Despite that, I am still constantly overstimulated and often triggered by my children, but that doesn't even come close to what it was like when they were babies.

My kids were both bad sleepers as babies, usually both waking up between eight to twelve times a night until they reached toddlerhood. Since they couldn't at least give me the courtesy of synchronizing their wake-up schedules, there were nights that I was up twenty-four times a night. After all that, they would then be awake for the day at 4:00 AM. By 9:00 AM, when most people were just arriving at work, I had already put in a five-hour day. And my day wouldn't end until around 6:00 PM when they went to bed.

Before you ask, yes, I tried everything. I tried sleep training, the cry-it-out method, the *never*-let-them-cry-it-out method. I adjusted their bedtime over and over. Nothing changed their evidently hard-wired sleep schedule. I remember one day being so exhausted that I put the kids in a corner of their playroom with a few of their favorite toys and made a tripwire of my own body by laying on the ground to form the "third wall" around them. I knew I'd wake up if one of them toddled across my body to where real danger could be. And then, knowing that, I let myself sleep.

Showers were a luxury I only got when the babies happened to have a "nap-overlap" or after they were in bed. Usually, by then, I was too exhausted to even rinse myself. I'd rather be dirty than bear the thought of having to look at my naked postpartum body or to hold my arms over my head long enough to wash my hair.

For years, I was a smelly, sleepy, irritable mess.

These days, I'm sleeping better and showering more often. But as far as exhaustion goes, I don't feel like things are much different from the way they were in the baby years. Old routines replaced new ones. Every step toward my kids' independence came along with new ways they needed me. I no longer have to change diapers, but I do have to check heinies to make sure they're properly wiped. I don't make midnight bottles anymore, but now I am the maker of lunches and the getter of snacks. Although my kids don't cry inexplicably anymore, I now know why they are crying, and somehow that's worse. My heart aches while they weep over a friend who rejected them or a bully at school who just won't leave them alone. I see their hearts break as they learn about injustice in the world, of poverty, sickness, and greed. I hold them as they learn what death is—first a fish, then a dog, then, eventually, a grandparent. I walk that tightrope of sharing my emotions so that they can see that I am human, too, while trying to be a beacon of strength and emotional stability for them.

I recognize that *this* labor, the emotional labor of loving children in a world that hurts, will only grow as they get older. Physically, they will need me less. Emotionally, they will need me more and more. Sometimes, they will need more than I have available to give.

As moms, we spend a lifetime giving more than we have. That exhaustion is so deep, so engrained. When we say, *I'm tired*, we speak paragraphs. Those words encapsulate the hundreds of times we choose to whisper when we want to scream. The sensation of being touched out and overstimulated but still holding our kids close because it's what they need. The ache of remembering who we used to be—a showered, well-fed, happy ghost of ourselves from another life, a ghost who we wouldn't know how to find these days even if we had the time to try.

The ache of remembering who we used to be—a showered, well-fed, happy ghost of ourselves from another life, a ghost who we wouldn't know how to find these days even if we had the time to try.

This is why I get so frustrated when I hear people give moms well-meaning but unhelpful advice like *go take a bubble bath or make a Target run*! Why are we expected to find rest and rejuvenation from silly, inconsequential things like that? Taking care of our hygiene and buying our groceries are basic human needs. Why are moms supposed to think of them as self-care?

Although I know that not everyone reading this book is a mom, some of you will be one day. Some of you will have friends who will be moms, and although you may be child-free by choice, you will still want to help those friends when they are lost and exhausted. You'll want to know the right things to say, the right ways to help. So, I want all of us, I *need* all of us, to understand the intersection of motherhood and self-care.

Bubble baths are lovely and grocery store trips are . . . fun? At least they're a break from hearing the word *Mommy* belted at you a hundred times (*if* you're lucky enough to make a trip to the store alone). But self-care cannot be found in glistening soap bubbles or the baking-goods aisle. Self-care, particularly for moms, is investing in, insisting on, and perpetually nurturing our needs.

But self-care cannot be found in glistening soap bubbles or the baking-goods aisle. Self-care, particularly for moms, is investing in, insisting on, and perpetually nurturing our needs.

We need alone time—time to reset and calm our nerves after a day of caring for everyone but ourselves. I truly believe we will lose our minds if we don't have those precious moments to hold at least a few uninterrupted thoughts in our heads.

We need to be able to take care of our physical bodies. We need regular showers, ones that don't include a toddler peering creepily at us through the glass door. We need opportunities to exercise, however little that may be. Even things like going on brief walks or doing a free Yoga class on YouTube can make a huge difference in our mental health and well-being. We need to be able to prepare nutritious meals for ourselves and actually have time to sit down and eat them.

We need *support*—people who recognize the struggle of parenting without a village and offer to be that village for us. It starts with our partners. I am so tired of hearing from moms who say that their spouses don't help around the house because "that's the wife's job." They crash on the couch after work and let their wives (who have been up since 5:00 AM with the kids and hasn't sat down yet today) cook dinner, clean up the kitchen, bathe the kids, and put them to bed, all because "they did their job already." We need partners who see us. We need family, friends, and neighbors who see us, too. If we can't have a village, we at least need a team, a team we can rely on for support, a team who anticipates our needs before we have to ask.

We need partners who see us. We need family, friends, and neighbors who see us, too. If we can't have a village, we at least need a team.

We need to feel safe to articulate our feelings and needs without having them invalidated, diminished, or criticized. That feels like such a bare minimum thing, but as most of us moms know, it seems to be a lot to ask. Society loves to tell moms we are selfish for needing more than self-care potato chips to survive. We ask for something that nourishes, something that fulfills and sticks to the ribs, and we're called ungrateful. *Why did you become a mom if you didn't want potato chips for the rest of your life?* As if they could sustain themselves on the crumbs we live off of.

Most of all, we need what I call the "self-hyphenates." They're all the words that begin with *self* and are followed by a hyphen. The self-hyphenates are things like self-worth, self-esteem, self-efficacy, self-confidence, self-respect, self-expression, and self-compassion.

- ***Self-worth:*** the sense of your own value as a person, determined not by other people but by your innate qualities.
- ***Self-esteem:*** a favorable impression of yourself and your abilities.
- ***Self-efficacy:*** the belief that certain things are within your control and that you know how to effectively manage and overcome them.
- ***Self-confidence:*** the certainty that you can trust yourself to handle various situations and challenges, believing that you can succeed.

- ***Self-respect:*** a belief that you are worthy of treating yourself with dignity and honor and that you deserve for others to treat you the same.
- ***Self-expression:*** the ability to express your thoughts, feelings, and ideas in a way that reflects your true identity and personality without fear or judgment or rejection.
- ***Self-compassion:*** the practice of treating yourself with kindness, understanding, and care during times of difficulty and acknowledging that you have imperfections and shortcomings without judging or criticizing yourself.

Building up the self-hyphenates takes time. It is not easy work, and to be honest with you, dear reader, we aren't always in a season when it's possible to work diligently on these things, but we can make tiny steps. When we prioritize self-care and grant ourselves the nourishment we deserve, we are, in essence, nurturing our *self-worth*. The act of investing in ourselves through self-care creates a ripple effect, and the growth of our *self-esteem* follows suit.

As our self-esteem grows, we become more courageous, being able to try new things that intimidate us or that we think we can't do. In doing these things and succeeding at them, we build *self-efficacy* and *self-confidence*. Confidence gives us the permission we need to stand up for ourselves, to insist on our needs being met. When we see the world responding to us with the dignity we deserve, we begin to develop a deep sense of *self-respect*.

When we see the world responding to us with the dignity we deserve, we begin to develop a deep sense of *self-respect*.

All these things build upon each other. They give us constant reminders that we are worthy, that we are capable and strong. Our belief in these things gives us the confidence to show up authentically—to engage in glorious *self-expression*, putting our truest nature on display without regard for what other people think. And when we do happen to disappoint or let down the people who matter to us, we reach into the well of self-worth and self-esteem we have built for ourselves and pull out a healthy dose of *self-compassion*. We let go of perfectionism. We release shame. We forgive ourselves, make amends, and move forward with grace.

We let go of perfectionism. We release shame. We forgive ourselves, make amends, and move forward with grace.

Although that process may take time, it is something you can begin right now. It starts with something as simple as choosing to put yourself first, just once. One small step, then another, then another. The more confident you become in your ability to invest in true self-care, the easier the path becomes.

This is what we need. Bubble baths won't cut it, though they are nice from time to time. Solo trips to the grocery store won't do, even though we will always take them when we can get them. Those are self-care potato chips—a nice little empty-calorie snack for your soul when you need something quick and convenient. They do not, and cannot, fill us up. As moms, as women, we deserve the things that truly nourish.

It's time for us to give ourselves permission to get wonderfully, unapologetically full.

Cultivate Your Truth Trench

- **You deserve more than superficial self-care.** Traditional self-care advice like bubble baths and solo grocery store trips are insufficient for moms dealing with deep exhaustion. Self-care for moms involves investing in, insisting on, and nurturing their needs on a fundamental level.
- **Your basic needs are nonnegotiable.** You deserve time to yourself to reset and calm your nerves, regular showers and physical exercise, nutritious meals, and a support system that recognizes your struggles and offers genuine help. Sensible self-care means insisting on these things.
- **Your emotional well-being matters.** Prioritize the development of self-hyphenates such as self-worth, self-esteem, self-efficacy, self-confidence, self-respect, self-expression, and self-compassion. Nurturing these traits takes time and effort but leads to profound personal growth and resilience.
- **Accept nothing less than what makes you full.** Potato chips are nice, but they will never fill you up. You must insist on being fulfilled in every aspect of your life. That means getting your physical, mental, emotional, relational, and spiritual needs met, and that is not up for debate.

Chapter Twenty-One

Cut Off the Arm to Save the Body

My first boyfriend was my high school sweetheart. We met on the speech and debate team, and I was instantly in love. We dated throughout high school and then in college. We got engaged at twenty-two, which was the obvious next step for two kids who had been dating for seven years.

By that time, we had been through a lot. Our relationship wasn't perfect, and I was an immature and very toxic version of myself back then. Still, he loved me. He treated me well, but I was young and ambitious and probably not ready to settle down. We were following the script of expectation, the relationship elevator that whisks you up, first with marriage, then children, then the mundane forever after. I was split in two—one woman who was ready for the conventional married life of a young, southern, Christian woman, and one who wanted the taste of freedom. My parents had raised me to the age of sixteen and passed me along to a wonderful boy who loved me, and from then, I was his. I had never been *mine*, and I wanted that desperately. I also had a few reasons to believe I wouldn't be happy with that boy forever.

He was conservative; I was liberal. He had a big, very close family, and I was an only child whose parents were my whole world. He viewed marriage through the lens of traditional gender roles and family dynamics, and I was applying to doctoral programs to become someone who would forever be addressed as *doctor*. His family really struggled with this, wondering how that boy's ego would handle hearing *Mr. and Dr. So and So* for the rest of his life. He was, in my humble opinion, too close with his mother. I say that gingerly. I have a son of my own now, and I want him to love me and be close to me forever. But I also want him to love his chosen spouse or partner more than me one day. I didn't get the impression that this boy's mom wanted the same for him. As he and I got older, closer, and more committed, it began to feel (at least in my very young mind) that she and I were *competing* with each other.

It was that last piece, the mother issue, that kept me skeptical about our future. I thought we might be able to overcome the other stuff, but having an antagonistic mother-in-law was just something I didn't think I could survive. Please don't misunderstand me, she was an absolutely wonderful person. Kind, generous, and welcoming. Everyone loved her and rightly so. Her only crime was clinging too closely to a boy who was ready to take a new leading lady in his life. As a mom myself now, that hits closer to home than I would have been able to understand back then. I understand it now, but I'm still glad I didn't stay.

I loved that boy. At least, the part of me who wanted the picture of a traditional marriage did. The other part, the part of me who understood that this marriage was going to be one that we had to white-knuckle our way through, wanted to run. And run, I did. I called off our engagement. If memory serves, it was about six weeks before the wedding. My family was supportive and unsurprised. They had been preparing for this, having understood that losing the deposits and down payments for the venue, the catering, and the rest was worth rescuing a daughter from a marriage that just wasn't right for her. Frankly, they had come to this realization long before I had. My closest friends, who were going to support me if this marriage was what I wanted but who knew deep down that it wasn't (despite my protestations otherwise), walked in step with me through the relief and the grief.

That boy's family, on the other hand, was in shock. They were heartbroken for their son, for us, for themselves. Like any loving parents who adore their children, they were protective of him, which meant they were very angry at me. His father called to tell me that I was dead to him. Their longtime family friends, whose daughters were going to be bridesmaids in the wedding, phoned my parents and called me some names I don't want to repeat. Other members of the family, ones whom I loved and had known since I was sixteen, said nothing. I knew I would never hear from them again.

I was going to miss them—all of them—especially the young ones, the little kids who I had known since they were babies and who felt like family to me. Losing them felt like cutting off an arm to save the rest of my body. It sucked. It sucked for me and for the arm. Gruesome but necessary.

Over the years, I have often thought back to that boy and his family. From what I have gathered here and there on Facebook, he met a beautiful girl not long after I called off our wedding, and they are married now. They have kids; they look happy. A portrait of the traditional American dream. I'm glad that boy got what he wanted and deserved.

It was years after we went separate ways until I ran into his family again. The father who I had loved, who told me I was dead to him. The too-attached mother who I also loved and who I do believe loved me at one time, too. The little brother, no longer little and suddenly far too grown. I exchanged pleasantries with the grown-ups. The little brother threw his arms around me, a precious and painful reminder that we had loved each other at one time. I had so much I wanted to say to them. To extend my apologies. To tell them I am so sorry their family became the innocent bystanders of my escape. To tell them I still loved them and missed them and maybe we could stay in touch? But sometimes, when you hurt someone to save yourself, you don't know how to start those conversations. They didn't ask to have an old scab picked off the wound right there in the middle of O'Charley's, so I said goodbye and left. That night, I cried myself to sleep for the first time in years.

Sometimes, self-care means amputating a part of your own body.

Sometimes, self-care means amputating a part of your own body. It means cutting off a part of you that just isn't working so that the rest of the body can function well. It hurts like hell. You feel every tear of muscle and flesh, every sinew. You may even get halfway through it and wonder if you've made a mistake, but by then it's too late to save it and you have to keep going. Besides, you know it's for the best. No one just chops off their arm without doing some real soul searching first. So, you keep going.

Hurting that boy, that family I had come to call my own, was terrible. I had my own pain to process. I also had to process the pain I knew I caused all of them—the people who had loved me as best they could since I was a kid myself. I have never regretted leaving that situation, but I do regret the collateral damage I left behind. And this is where I really need you to hear me. I am talking to the unmarried women, the ones who think they might be ready to settle down but have some doubts. I'm also talking to the married women who have thought of leaving a troubled marriage but the idea of the hurting your spouse keeps you rooted where you are.

I'm talking to you as a woman who fled—twice. I'd fled an engagement and saved myself from a life I knew I didn't want, and I fled again, many years later, from a marriage that made me miserable, a marriage that, thankfully, I found my way back to. It's important to me that you understand this, because I am not here to tell everyone to just up and leave their spouses or partners because something feels "off." What I *am* here to tell you is that sometimes, amputation is necessary. Sometimes, it is the only way to save yourself.

I need you to understand that you will survive the pain you feel if you choose to not settle down, to say no to the engagement ring, to contact the divorce attorney.

I need you to understand that you will survive the pain you feel if you choose to not settle down, to say no to the engagement ring, to contact the divorce attorney. I need you to know that the greatest act of self-care you can make when it comes to your romantic relationship is to leave if it is no longer in your best interest to stay. I need you to love yourself enough to know that their comfort is not more important than yours.

This goes not just for our spouses or partners but also for our extended families. You have permission to go no contact with anyone,

You have permission to go no contact with anyone, even your own family, if they are causing you more harm than good.

even your own family, if they are causing you more harm than good. It's always good to try to reconcile family relationships when you can through boundary setting, open communication, or even therapy. But you can't control other people. You can't force them to change if they don't want to. By the same token, they can't control you or expect you to change to suit their needs. They also can't expect you to stay around them if their actions, words, or choices make you uncomfortable. You are allowed to release those people who can't be what you need them to be or who refuse to accept you as your authentic self.

The last thing I need you to know is that the people you say goodbye to, the relationships you amputate for your own good, they will be okay eventually, too.

That boy, that family, they are doing great. They found their way to the life that was meant for them—a life that was not supposed to include me. And for that, I call our relationship a success even though it failed. The relationship served its purpose: to push us all to the paths we were really meant to be on. I need you to see that and know it.

We all survive the amputations in the end.

Cultivate Your Truth Trench

- **Amputations are always sad, but they're sometimes necessary.** Sometimes self-care means making difficult decisions to protect your own well-being, even if it means causing pain to others. Understand that amputation, metaphorically speaking, may be necessary to ensure personal growth and happiness.
- **Collateral damage is often part of it.** Accept the reality of collateral damage when making decisions that prioritize self-preservation. While leaving may be necessary for personal growth, it may also cause pain and upheaval for loved ones involved. You can honor and hold space for their pain while also doing what you need to do to protect your peace.
- **It can hurt and still be right.** Trust yourself enough to prioritize your own happiness and well-being. It's okay to leave relationships that no longer serve your best interests, even if it means facing temporary discomfort or uncertainty. Feeling pain doesn't mean it was the wrong decision; it means you haven't let yourself go numb.
- **It didn't fail, it only ended.** Even though relationships may end, it doesn't diminish their significance or value. Endings are opportunities for growth and redirection toward paths that align more closely with your true self. You are allowed to grieve the end without calling it a failure.

Chapter Twenty-Two

Parenting the Inner Child

Inside every woman is a little girl who remembers.

She remembers what it was like to be unselfconscious. To run through the grass in her bare feet, feeling the morning dew on her skin. She remembers what it felt like to trust everyone, to believe in the natural goodness of others. She remembers eating what she wanted without worrying about going up a jeans size. She remembers how to *play*.

She existed before the world taught her that those things are childish. Before the people who were supposed to love her the most broke her tiny, unready heart. Before a society that transforms fearless little girls into compliant, conventional women. Before she learned that the only type of play that matters is playing by the rules.

I think a lot of people over-romanticize childhood when they speak about the *inner child*. They speak about this child as if it exists in the past tense. They imagine that the inner child was a happy, if naive, idealistic version of themselves who eventually faded away with adulthood. Their version of the inner child only knew happiness and fun.

This idea of the inner child is wrong in almost every way. The inner child is not a ghost of the past. She exists with us in the present, she is incorporated into our very being. And, perhaps with the exception of very few, very fortunate people, the inner child is not the bearer of only happy memories. For many of us, the inner child carries trauma: trauma of neglect, of abuse, of shame, or of profound longing. Our inner child carries pain that we buried when it became too painful or too inconvenient to feel.

Our inner child carries pain that we buried when it became too painful or too inconvenient to feel.

But that little girl, that inner child, remembers.

She is in need of a parent. A mother who shows her the unconditional love and positive regard she deserved. The only person who can be that mother to that little girl is you. This is not to say that your own mother didn't do a great job or isn't *still* doing a great job. It means that your mother was parenting you while also parenting her own inner child, whether she said so or not. She was ruled by her own feelings and needs. She loved you the best she could while trying desperately to love herself. If you were lucky, she taught you what good mothering looks like. (Mom, if you're reading this, I consider myself the luckiest.) She gave you the template and the tools for being a good mom. If you were unlucky, perhaps the best thing she gave you was an example of how *not* to parent a child.

Whether you are a mom these days or not, you still have the hard, lifelong work of parenting your inner child ahead of you. Self-care is loving that inner child enough to be her devoted mother, to show her the love she deserved from a world that cuts little girls down before they have a chance to bloom.

Self-care is loving that inner child enough to be her devoted mother, to show her the love she deserved from a world that cuts little girls down before they have a chance to bloom.

The self-care of loving your inner child means parenting, and perhaps *re-parenting*, that child who lives within you. It is hard work. It's work that, honestly, you should be doing with a therapist if that is accessible to you. I can't speak about parenting your inner child from a therapeutic perspective, but I can talk to you about it as it relates to self-care.

Your inner child is not child*ish*. She is child*like*.

Your inner child is not child*ish*. She is child*like*. She represents, and is, the things we most commonly think of in children. She is vulnerable—experiencing emotions deeply—and very sensitive to criticism or rejection. She is playful—curious, creative, and imaginative, open to new experiences. She is authentic—expressing herself with honesty and not hiding herself from the world. She has strong intuition—knowing the difference between right and wrong and caring deeply about fairness. Most importantly, she has a need for love and validation. She needs to feel connected to others and accepted for who she is.

She also holds on to the pain, hurt, and trauma from your childhood. As a result, she may have developed some coping strategies and defense mechanisms that make all the lovely characteristics I just listed seem dull or nonexistent. She may have been criticized too much as a child, so now she doesn't open up to people like she used to. Maybe she wasn't listened to or believed when she spoke about bad things that adults were doing to her, and now she doesn't trust her own memory or experiences. Perhaps, most heartbreakingly of all, she was told that she was unlovable, a burden, a mistake. So, she doesn't seek the love that she deserves, accepting instead the kind of "love" that hurts her because at least that lines up with what she's been made to believe about herself.

I'm going to speak to the moms in the room for a second. Moms, what would you do if you were watching, day by day, all the beautiful and sparkling things about your delightfully unique children start to disappear? If you saw the light leaving their eyes, their interest and curiosity about the world beginning to shrink? If you saw them withdrawing from love and acceptance, and seeking out things that harm them instead? You would do absolutely anything in your power to heal their wounds, right? Wouldn't you stop at nothing to reignite that spark, that incredible childlike wonder? Of course you would. You're a good mom.

To the non-moms, I trust that if you picked up this book, you possess the kind of empathetic spirit that can understand that feeling, even though you don't have kids. You are smart and kind. You are a good person. You would never let someone else's light (especially a child's) go dim.

If we understand that this is what a living, breathing child would need, it should be easy to understand that our own inner child needs the same, yet we struggle. We dismiss our inner child. We gaslight her. We push her away because she makes us feel uncomfortable or ashamed—her big feelings are just too much for us to handle.

Self-care means bringing to our inner child all the love and compassion we would bring to a living child, being the parent she still needs today. In its most basic form, self-care of our inner child means taking action on her behalf. This means making her feel safe by providing for her basic needs. This means taking her to the doctor or calling a friend or a therapist when emotional support is needed. Do you go to the doctor when you are ill, or do you decide to muscle through it? Are you seeking therapy if it's accessible or doing your own personal growth at home if it's not? Or are you suppressing all your feelings and letting yourself slowly wither away? Your inner child is watching and discerning her worth based on your actions. When you get yourself the things that you need to be physically, mentally, and emotionally healthy, you tell her that she is worthy of love and safety.

Your inner child is watching, and discerning her worth based on your actions. When you get yourself the things that you need to be physically, mentally, and emotionally healthy, you tell her that she is worthy of love and safety.

Self-care of our inner child also means taking *loving actions* toward her. Because your inner child is where your intuition lives, it is so important to listen to the things she is telling you. You have experienced this tug of intuition from your inner child. Perhaps you called it your gut instinct. We often dismiss our gut instincts. They are emotionally driven, derived from what is *felt* instead of what is *observed*, and therefore, we count them as inconsequential. But these feelings-driven intuitions are important. When we love our inner child, we listen to her feelings. We want to understand why she feels what she feels, and by listening, we show that we trust her.

If we trust her, then we take action when she tells us how she feels. When she says, *I don't trust that person*, we ask her why and give her time and space to answer. Once we understand, we take a step back until she tells us she feels more comfortable. When she says, *I am tired and feeling overwhelmed*, we give her compassion. We may not be able to give her the rest she needs right away because we have adult responsibilities that we must attend to.

When we love our inner child, we listen to her feelings. We want to understand why she feels what she feels, and by listening, we show that we trust her.

What we *can* do is assure her that we will get her the rest she needs soon, when our responsibilities are taken care of. We establish trust with her by honoring our word and giving her the rest that she needs.

Self-care of our inner child means being curious and open-minded about her pain. Parenting her involves acknowledging and validating her past experiences and emotions and working to release any negative beliefs and patterns that may have developed as a result. It involves becoming aware of her triggers and learning to respond to them with compassion and understanding rather than reacting from a place of fear or hurt.

My inner child has a deep rejection wound. In therapy, I am working hard to understand where that wound originated and how my choices have allowed the wound to fester instead of heal. Part of self-care for me, and my inner child, is understanding that *I* struggle with rejection because *she* does. I am learning to have compassion toward myself when I am triggered by real or perceived rejection because I know those feelings are coming from a vulnerable little girl who just wants to be loved. And in helping her heal from the wounds of rejection that marked her so long ago, I am healing myself, too.

Self-care is surrounding my inner child with truth trenches. Encompassing her with the truth about who she is and what she deserves.

Self-care is surrounding my inner child with truth trenches. Encompassing her with the truth about who she is and what she deserves. I am the mama bear, standing in front of my cub with the truth so that the lies of this world cannot get to her. The lies that tell her she is a burden, she is unlovable, she is not pretty enough, or smart enough, not *enough enough enough* . . . cannot get through to her when she is enveloped in truth.

She learns to love herself fiercely because I love her that way.

I love *myself* that way.

Fiercely.

Cultivate Your Truth Trench

- **Your inner child is sacred.** Your inner child represents the innocent, curious, and vulnerable aspects of childhood that shaped your personality and perception. Our Western culture does a great job rooting those little girls out of us, but they are always there.
- **Your inner child carries your deepest wounds.** Your inner child may carry unresolved trauma from childhood experiences, including neglect, abuse, shame, or longing. Self-care is found in acknowledging her feelings and understanding how they shape your emotions and behaviors in the present.
- **Listen to her, and trust what she tells you.** Cultivate a trusting relationship with your inner child by listening to her intuition and honoring her feelings. Validate her instincts and emotions by responding with compassion and understanding to her needs and concerns.
- **Be the parent your inner child deserves.** Surround your inner child with a supportive environment of truth and love, reinforcing positive beliefs about self-worth and deservingness. Practice self-love fiercely, modeling the unconditional acceptance and validation your inner child needs to thrive.

Chapter Twenty-Three
Riddles

A riddle for you: What is the one sentence that will make the happiest woman on earth sob with grief and the saddest woman on earth exclaim with joy?

The answer? "This, too, shall pass."

Originally, I planned to use that riddle to speak about the joys and sorrows of motherhood—the way that being a mom somehow gives and takes in equal measure, the way we yearn for the independence we had before children while at the same time dreading the day that the independence returns to us. But as I've written my way through this book, one glaring realization I've had is that this riddle, this symbol of the transitory, joyful, and fearful nature of life, applies to us all.

As a mother, of course, I feel this in every way possible. The greatest joy and the biggest sorrow of my life is knowing that one day my children will grow up. I am not ashamed to admit that I look forward to that day. On the days that I feel sad and lonely, missing my old self and my precious independence, I very much look forward to having them grow up and leave the house. That said, on the happy days, the ones when my home is filled with cuddles and laughter, I am tormented by the thought that one day I will reach for them and not find a chubby arm to grab. One day my ears will ache for the sound of their nasally little voices. This is the great conflict of motherhood. It is beautiful and sparkling. Lonely and dark. I have to hold space for myself to accept this juxtaposition, this great irony, to remind myself that I am allowed to feel both at the same time, allowed to feel every moment, the blissful and the bleak.

I have to hold space for myself to accept this juxtaposition, this great irony, to remind myself that I am allowed to feel both at the same time, allowed to feel every moment, the blissful and the bleak.

This feeling of enjoying the good while dreading the bad, or persevering through the hard while looking forward to the easy, isn't unique to my role as a mother. It finds its way into every role I have as a woman, as a human being. I daydream about retiring with Charlie one day, traveling the world untethered to the demands of jobs that stopped inspiring us years ago. At the same time, I know I will miss work life, having career ambitions, and leaving my mark on the world.

As a social media personality, I sometimes hate putting my face and my ideas on the internet every day. I hate having my appearance, my intelligence, and my worth criticized by people who don't know me—by the scoffers who would rather put people down than raise themselves up. Those broken souls refuse to go to therapy and heal the way they need to, so I go to therapy to learn how to cope with the way their brokenness gets to me. I also know that one day, when I memorialize all my social media accounts and sign out, I will mourn the village I tried so hard to create for women like me, the kindness my community showed me, and the people who educated and inspired me, who made me better.

I swear at my ornery dog every time she gets the zoomies in our bed while we are trying to sleep, then I remember that, in her old age, I'll miss those goddamn zoomies. I love watching my parents love on my children, giving them the grandparents I never had, and I realize with an ache in my throat that one day my kids will lose them. I grow tired of chauffeuring my kids all over God's green earth, then consider that one day they'll be driving themselves, and I won't be able to keep them safe under my protective wings.

Everything has a season. *It all shall pass:* the good and the bad, the difficult and the easy. When it comes to my role within my family, I have to keep this perspective close to heart, to remember that everything is transitory. Even the things that feel so hard, so heavy, will be things that I miss one day; the things that feel easy and light right now might bring sorrow one day. A weird and oft-unspoken part of self-care is learning not to get too carried away by any of it; learning how to love fully and authentically while also knowing how to let go and letting myself feel every hard or uncomfortable feeling without letting it destroy me.

Everything has a season. *It all shall pass:* the good and the bad, the difficult and the easy.

That means taking time to appreciate the good things in the bad times, because the good things will leave with the bad. It also means not losing hope in the bad times, because when the bad times end, we will need to have something left in the tank to enjoy the good with. It means learning not to cling too tightly and remembering how quickly it all will pass like sand through desperate fingers.

Whatever you're going through, dear reader, *this, too, shall pass.* Whatever that means for you in that present moment, I hope you know you're not alone. Hold space for yourself to feel it all. And when the time comes, let it go.

Self-care is holding loosely.

Cultivate Your Truth Trench

- **In all things, maintain perspective.** Understand that both joy and sorrow are temporary and part of the human experience. This attitude helps you stay present in the joys of life and not become too defeated in the sorrows.
- **You are a beautiful soul, filled with contradictions.** Allow yourself to experience conflicting emotions simultaneously, such as yearning for independence while cherishing moments with loved ones. Life is beautiful and messy. You're allowed to feel several things at once. And your feelings are sacred.
- **Self-care is not clinging too tightly.** Learn to hold on to experiences and relationships loosely, understanding that attachment can bring both joy and pain, and allow yourself to let go when necessary.
- **Feel fully, without letting your emotions overpower you.** Allow yourself to feel every emotion deeply without letting it consume or destroy you, holding space for yourself to experience the full spectrum of human emotions while not reveling or sinking into any one, whether good or bad.

SECTION IV
Lunch Break:
Self-Care in Our Careers and Workplace

Chapter Twenty-Four

Mad Men

If this is a man's world, maybe we should let them have it. We'll build our own instead.

I've spent a lot of my career in male-dominated spaces. The majority of my graduate school professors were men. My thesis and dissertation committees were composed entirely of men. When I finished my degree, I accepted a position as the director of cognitive science at a company that focused primarily in STEM (science, technology, engineering, and math), and there, of course, my colleagues were mostly men.

The only position I've ever had that *wasn't* woefully male dominated was as a sales associate at Victoria's Secret during undergrad. You'd think that would be a safe place for women, but it wasn't. At least once per shift a man twice my age would shove a tower of lingerie into my arms and say, "You're the same size as my wife. Go try these on for me so I can see how she would look in them." Of course, I always said no and was pleased that, according to Victoria's Secret's policy, I could quickly have those men escorted out of the store. But still, you can only handle so much of these sorts of propositions in a day, especially when you're barely twenty years old and just trying to do your job.

In my now going on twenty years working in spaces that cater mostly to the needs and whims of men, I've seen a lot of complete buffoonery from the self-proclaimed "stronger sex"—a lot of fragility, too, now that I think of it. I'm going to share some stories with you because I know that I have never once in my life had an original experience. I know these stories will sound frustratingly familiar to you, too.

I have found that, in academic spaces like colleges and graduate schools, you mostly see the pandering, patriarchal form of sexism and misogyny that higher education supposedly despises. I didn't notice a lot of fragility in those men, which I assume is because they were "the elites." They held the prestige and the power. Hard to be fragile when you're the one who holds the keys. My department was comprised mostly of female doctoral students, which was wonderful! These were very limited, highly coveted positions in which your degree was entirely paid for by the school. It was encouraging to see that the faculty had decided to give those prized positions to women instead of men. But soon, I found that the veneer of fairness and equality was just that. A mirage. A cover.

When my dissertation advisor and I were preparing for my first invited talk at a conference, he said, "Could you buy yourself a pair of glasses to wear when you're there? It would make you look more professional." When I asked why glasses would make me look "more professional," he stammered and said, "Uh, well, you know. You have long hair, and you wear makeup. I just think, you know, people might think you're an airhead. They won't take you seriously." When I pointed out that I was invited to speak at this conference based on my merits and that my work speaks for itself, he had nothing to say, just suggested that I try to "make yourself look a little smarter."

I can't forget to mention the sexual innuendo and inappropriate touches from male faculty, the kind of behavior that always seems to accompany men who hold the power, who stand between you and your dreams.

I can't forget to mention the sexual innuendo and inappropriate touches from male faculty, the kind of behavior that always seems to accompany men who hold the power, who stand between you and your dreams.

Professional life wasn't much better. I found that men in professional settings, compared to academic ones, seemed to be more of the fragile variety. Sexism shows up in many forms, and fragility is one of them. Whereas the men from academia had more education and knowledge than I did, men in professional settings often found themselves less educated and knowledgeable than me—at least when it came to my area of expertise. Companies hired me because they needed someone with my expertise to counsel them, yet I found myself constantly at odds with the very men who hired me. The CEO of the STEM start up company I worked for had a degree in sales. Although I was hired to bring my unique knowledge of human cognition and emotion to the table, the CEO would frequently argue with me on these very topics, as though he knew more about them than me. It was more than mansplaining. It was argumentative, patronizing, and infuriating. He was a good man, a kind man in every other way. But my education and expertise seemed to be a constant stumbling block for him.

One of the worst moments at that job was when I came to him about sexual harassment I was experiencing from a male superior in our office. It had been going on for months by then. This superior was the gatekeeper between me and the resources I needed to do my job (access to time from team members, money, software applications I needed). He would frequently deny me access to those things unless I demurred to him in whatever ways he desired. I was falling behind on my deadlines, beginning to look like I was bad at my job. When I approached the CEO about what was going on, asking for him to intercede on my behalf, the conversation went . . . poorly. It ended with me sobbing while he screamed in my face, "The only people I give a shit about are my investors. Period! I don't give a shit about this, or about him, or about you. I give a shit about my investors and that they are happy. End of story!"

Startups are hard. CEOs have employees to pay and the constant pressure of failure nipping at their neck. In those beginning years, you eat solely out of the hands of stingy investors who may or may not show up with the checkbook. I understood (still understand) his stress. I even understand how his stress led to this completely inappropriate outburst. But understanding where the outburst came from didn't change the depth of the pain it caused me, the anguish I felt over turning to someone who had felt like a father figure to me (I know, I know) and who betrayed me when I needed his help the most.

While at the same startup, a male client from a big and well-known firm in New York followed me down the hall to show me the restroom and pinned me against the wall, trying to kiss me. My organization did nothing about this because "this was an important client." You know, no need to ruffle feathers.

I've sat at corporate lunches and listened to men tell blonde jokes, brunette jokes, airhead jokes. Heard them say despicable things about their wives and was told to learn to take a joke when I dissented. It was a boys' club, and somehow, I had "earned" a seat at the table. At the tender age of twenty-eight, I was learning what it meant to exist as a woman in the workplace.

I eventually left that job and started my own business (more on that later). I've continued to do freelance and consulting work in my spare time and have found that the workplace hasn't changed much. I recently asked my social media community to share stories with me of the ways they have experienced sexism or misogyny in the workplace. Within hours I had *thousands* of comments from women sharing horror stories of how they have been treated by the men they work with. Most of them hard to read. All of them infuriating.

When I asked these women why they chose to stay silent in those work environments, the most common answer was "because I was afraid of retaliation." They feared losing their jobs or being overlooked for opportunities. They feared putting a target on their backs that would further escalate their mistreatment at work. They feared being labeled as the uptight bitch who never developed a sense of humor. They feared these things because they knew they were real.

Workplaces were not made with us in mind. And if there is anything we learned from the Me Too movement, it's that whatever progress we had made to shape workplaces into our image, it was only a veneer. Mind you, *we* already knew that, but the men didn't. For me, Me Too served as a wake-up call. For perhaps the first time, I realized my experiences at work weren't unique. I wasn't the only woman gritting my teeth through the workday, enduring the insufferable antics of entitled men. Most importantly, I discovered that it wasn't that something was wrong with me. When *that many* women come forward speaking about the sexism, harassment,

Workplaces were not made with us in mind. And if there is anything we learned from the Me Too movement, it's that whatever progress we had made to shape workplaces into our image, it was only a veneer.

When *that many* women come forward speaking about the sexism, harassment, and discriminatory behavior in the workplace, it can't be all of us who are the problem.

and discriminatory behavior in the workplace, it can't be all of us who are the problem.

The problem is the workplace and the men who have managed to maintain the status quo. The problem is the fact that fragile men are threatened by powerful, self-governing women. The problem, as I see it, is only solvable by us.

I understand our fears of speaking out, of demanding workplaces that keep us safe, healthy, and accommodated. The fear of retaliation is real, it's oppressive. But is it kind to ourselves to go to work every day in fear? Is it self-loving to tolerate the fragility and entitlement of men at the expense of our peace and well-being? Perhaps, more importantly, is it loving to our daughters, to our granddaughters, our nieces, our goddaughters to not do *something*? Is this the type of workplace we want them to inherit?

Self-care in the workplace means standing up for ourselves. It means being assertive and proactive in demanding safe and equitable treatment. This includes setting clear boundaries and communicating them effectively to colleagues and managers. It means advocating for ourselves when it comes to pay, promotions, and other career opportunities. It means unapologetically speaking up when we experience or witness discrimination or harassment in the workplace and taking advantage of any available resources or support systems to address these issues. Lastly, it means creating and nurturing workplaces that are made in *our* image. Over the next few chapters, I'll show you examples of how it's done.

Cultivate Your Truth Trench

- **Sexism is real; be loud about it.** There are those who claim that sexism is dead and equality has been achieved, but we know this to be untrue. Give yourself permission to be loud about mistreatment you and others receive in the workplace, from subtle biases to overt harassment.
- **Never take a back seat to any man's fragility or entitlement.** When you can do it safely, confront the fragility and entitlement displayed by some men in professional settings, particularly when their behavior undermines your expertise, boundaries, and well-being.
- **Self-advocacy is self-care.** Embrace assertiveness and proactive communication to demand safe, equitable treatment in the workplace, and speak out against discrimination and harassment. Standing up for yourself shows yourself and others what you are worth.
- **You are more powerful than you think.** Take an active role in fostering inclusive workplaces that reflect and accommodate the needs of women, challenging traditional norms, and advocating for systemic change to create environments where all employees feel safe, respected, and valued. This is what you and all women deserve.

Chapter Twenty-Five

Sometimes, the Customer Is Just Wrong

That last chapter was a little heavy. Perhaps a palate cleanser is in order?

I want to tell you a story about the greatest and most terrifying moment I had while running my small business. It's last-chapter *adjacent*? I want to show you a hopefully empowering example of how we create workplaces in our image, the image of women like you and me, but this time without any men in the story.

You're welcome.

In 2016, I founded an online baby boutique named The Sensible Mama. It was a retail store that sold the essentials like diaper bags, pacifiers, sippy cups, and more. A few years later, I launched my own line of luxury diaper bags and accessories called LYMIA BRAND. Both businesses steadily grew as the years went on, and I managed to carve out a nice little family business for myself.

We gained a ton of new customers during the pandemic while everyone was trapped in their homes and in need of provisions. It was really the first time that my business was exposed to a swarm of new customers who hadn't been longtime community members of mine. As a result of the influx of sales and the need for additional inventory and shipping procedures, I purchased a warehouse and staffed it up. I now had people depending on me. A lease to pay for. More pressure and responsibilities than ever.

Through my online community, I had fostered a culture of kindness and empathy. This culture found its way to every facet of the business. We treated customers with respect, committing ourselves to radical customer service. In turn, the customers treated us the same. They were friendly, understanding when things went wrong. Impossibly forgiving. So, it was a shock to me when one of our new customers, who didn't know anything about our community or values, became a constant source of disrespect and anxiety with my staff.

She was one of *those* customers. Everything was a problem. Even when her order was handled perfectly—shipped out the same day, handled impeccably by the mail carriers, and arrived within two days of the order date (no easy feat when you offer free shipping and don't have a fleet of delivery vans like Amazon), she still complained. My customer support staff bent over backward to make her happy. They sent her replacements. Gave partial refunds when she was unhappy. Called her on the phone to give her the personal touch she seemed to need. Eventually, with all the discounts and free product she was getting, plus the shipping fees we incurred and the sunk time it took to handle her issues, we were actually losing money on this customer.

But (but!), she was a regular customer. She was also a loud customer—someone we were sure would blast us on social media if we didn't appease her every whim. These days, your "social media credit score" as a small business is everything. I didn't think we could afford whatever story she would cook up about us, so I asked my staff to be patient with her and just try to keep her happy.

We tried. We tried so damn hard. But like most people with her sort of temperament, she eventually pushed us just an inch too far. She demanded to speak on the phone with the woman who was the head of my customer support staff at the time. I told my employee she did not have to take the call. It could be handled over email, or I could take the call instead. She insisted that she could handle it, and off she went to take the phone call. From the moment the call began, this customer was on a mission to do some damage. Maybe even get someone fired. You know those people who can't be bothered to be kind to the people serving their meals or cleaning their hotel rooms? It was like that—an utter disdain for "the help," as she put it. My employee was a mom, a hard worker, a friend. She was one of the strongest women I knew. But by the time that call ended, she was furious, humiliated, and shaking. She said the customer would like to speak to me, so I got on the phone.

Just like that, the customer switched her tone. She was cordial, if curt, but at least spoke to me like I was a human being. I was immediately agitated that she felt I was deserving of respect but my employee was not. She went on to lie to me about how badly my employee treated her. When I told her I had a hard time believing her story because I was in the room during the phone call, she became angry, belligerent. And when she realized she wasn't going to get what she wanted out of me, she escalated things further. She threatened to "expose us" on social media (I was expecting that) and to get lawyers

I was immediately agitated that she felt I was deserving of respect but my employee was not.

involved (that I was *not* expecting) if I didn't have my employee apologize to her privately and publicly. "The customer is *always right*!" she shouted as she made her threats.

She forfeited the benefit of the doubt when she made a nonissue into something personal, into something that belittled someone who was under my protection, the umbrella of my care.

The thing is, the customer is not always right. At least not in my book. She crossed the line when she humiliated my employee and treated her like gum she'd stepped in. She forfeited the benefit of the doubt when she made a nonissue into something personal, into something that belittled someone who was under my protection, the umbrella of my care.

I drew in a deep breath, gathered my courage, and told her that, effective immediately, she was banned from my store. She would be IP banned and her shipping address flagged. We would no longer respond to her customer service inquiries. I heard her shouting at me as I, more calmly than I anticipated, pressed End Call.

There are enough workplaces where women feel unsafe, enough spaces where women feel unprotected at best and preyed upon at worst. As a woman-owned business, the barest of bare minimum that I can provide for my female staff is to keep them safe—to show them that someone gives a damn about their dignity and mental health.

There are enough workplaces where women feel unsafe, enough spaces where women feel unprotected at best and preyed upon at worst.

From that moment on, I decided to go *Boondocks Saints* when it came to my business. No! I went Keyser Soze from *The Usual Suspects*. You know that scene where the bad guys hold Soze's whole family hostage, threatening to kill them all if he didn't do what they said? You remember what he did? *He shot his whole family himself.* That was me in this moment. I would risk letting this person try (*try*) to kill my business that I loved dearly before I made my employee bend the knee to someone who humiliated her. I would be willing to lose sales, lose my reputation, whatever, if it meant defending and protecting my female employees from being harassed on the job. It would become a mindset I would hold on to for the rest of the time I ran that business.

Sometimes, self-care in the workplace means fundamentally refusing to let the bad guy win (because, yes, customers can indeed be the bad guy). Sometimes it means taking a good look at who you really care about and what they are worth and making a hard decision on their behalf. Banning that customer risked doing harm to my business, but the far worse damage would have been throwing my employee under the bus for the sake of the almighty dollar. In that moment, self-care meant sticking to my ethics, standing up for the people under my care, and being prepared to face the consequences.

In that moment, self-care meant sticking to my ethics, standing up for the people under my care, and being prepared to face the consequences.

As these things tend to go, word got out about what I did. And you know what? We got more sales as a result. It turns out that women love a story of a business owner sticking up for her female employees. Sadly, they love the story because it is rare.

Self-care is bizarre and paradoxical at times. Sometimes, the things we have to do to take care of ourselves in the long run don't make sense in the present. I am a business owner who believes fervently that women deserve to be safe and respected at work. Allowing someone to disrespect my employee would have been in conflict with those convictions. I feel like there are some misguided "self-care gurus" out there who would say that self-care in this situation would have meant smoothing things over with the rude customer for the sake of peace, to keep the scathing Yelp review at bay. But honestly? That route, in the long run, would have done me more harm than good. Nobody likes doing things that clash with their values. It feels *bad* to throw another person under the bus to save yourself, even if you can do a good job rationalizing it to yourself and to others. Self-care may mean leaning into the brave but fearful reality that standing up for what you know is right can, sometimes, have consequences. It means upholding your values, your dignity, and your identity over whatever consequences there may be because in the long run, you will recover from most of those external consequences. You may never fully heal from compromising your internal needs.

Self-care may mean leaning into the brave but fearful reality that standing up for what you know is right can, sometimes, have consequences.

You may never fully heal from compromising your internal needs.

Whatever your role is at work, whether you are the owner, the team lead or the intern, the store manager, or the sales associate, you can choose to put your convictions first. Your convictions are valid; they matter. You have so much more power than you know. Power to create change. Power to protect those who need it. Power to do the right thing even when it is scary.

Self-care is unapologetically and unflinchingly standing in that power. It is creating workplaces in our own image.

Workplaces that work for us.

Cultivate Your Truth Trench

- **We all contribute to the culture.** You don't have to be the boss or CEO to help create and sustain a workplace culture that prioritizes kindness, empathy, and respect. Sometimes, all it takes is one person setting the tone. Recognize your influence and authority within your workplace, whether as an owner, manager, or team member, and use it to advocate for positive change, protect vulnerable employees, and promote a culture of empowerment and respect.
- **Disrespect is never okay.** It is normal to fear speaking up when disrespect happens because no one wants to lose their job. But sensible self-care is being fully convinced that you deserve a safe and respectful workplace and striving to create that kind of environment for yourself and your fellow employees.
- **Sometimes, there are consequences for doing what's right.** Standing up for your convictions may bring consequences, but it is important to prioritize your internal needs and values over external pressures or potential repercussions. You will survive the consequences of standing up for your convictions, but the effect of betraying your own standards is hard to overcome.
- **Empowering yourself empowers others.** Believe it or not, there are always people looking to you for an example of how to handle challenging circumstances. Standing up for yourself and others by demanding respectful and humane treatment empowers others to do the same.

Chapter Twenty-Six

The Reaching Hand

I reached back to another woman coming up the mountain behind me, and instead of letting me hoist her up, she grabbed my hand and yanked me down.

Shortly after starting my business, someone who followed me on social media asked to pick my brain about her business idea. I was committed to empowering other women to start businesses of their own and was excited that someone finally wanted my help. I made myself available to hear her idea and hopefully give her some useful guidance.

She didn't tell me the name of her business or what type of business it was going to be. That struck me as odd, but it's not uncommon for people to not share those things until they are set in stone. I tried not to think too much of it. She picked my brain about how to start an LLC, what kinds of certifications she would need, how to secure retailer agreements. She wanted to know how to set up a Shopify store, how to integrate PayPal, how to offer flexible payment plans (and is that a good idea?). I helped her as much as I could and wished her much success.

Imagine my surprise when, a few months later, she revealed her *online baby boutique* to the world. Her business's name, her branding, her website, everything seemed eerily similar to mine. She had taken my free guidance and created a business that would directly compete with mine and hadn't even bothered to make her business a significant departure from my own. I was disgruntled and maybe a little angry, but I tried to brush it off. After all, competition isn't necessarily a bad thing in a free market, and I still sincerely wanted her to succeed.

Over time, though, things got more and more questionable. She onboarded all of the same brands I carried in my store—even ones I had discovered on my own that weren't in the other boutiques. She began lifting copy off my website and putting it on her own. I knew this for certain because, at the time, I was writing my own copy. Once, she so blatantly stole my copy that she included the same typo on her website that I had on mine. Every unique thing I did to make my business stand out from the crowd, she copied it. I spent a lot of time listening to Billie Eilish's song "Copycat" during that season of my life.

All of that could have been brushed off as petty, inconsequential when the bomb dropped. I discovered from people within my online community that she and her friends had infiltrated my business's Facebook chat group and were bad-mouthing me to my customers. They also tried to poach my customers, begging them (in private DMs) to shop with her instead of me because she really needed to grow her business. When I went on to launch LYMIA BRAND, she and her friends flooded my page with negative reviews and blasted my name all over social media. She began throwing shade at me and my business on her social media pages, directly and indirectly putting me down to prop herself up.

I was heartbroken and furious. I had done nothing wrong to this woman, and she used me for whatever I could offer her and then made me her enemy.

I was heartbroken and furious. I had done nothing wrong to this woman, and she used me for whatever I could offer her and then made me her enemy.

As women, we learn to be nice even when it hurts. We are told to *take the high road, turn the other cheek, don't stoop to their level.* That's what is becoming of a woman, of course. Don't make waves. Be polite. Hold your tongue. So, that's what I did. I kept my head down and kept working on my own business, trusting that one day karma would come for her. And eventually it did, but it wouldn't be until years later. In the interim, I spent a lot of time licking the wounds of betrayal and wondering if justice would ever be served.

But I did learn my lesson.

What I took away from this experience was that there is a difference between niceness and kindness. Since society tells us that "good" women are nice and helpful, we feel pressure to go above and beyond, even at our own expense, to help others. In my effort to be *nice,* I hadn't done my due diligence. I didn't ask her what her plans were for her business before giving her my help. I gave her more time than I had to give, thinking that it was rude or gate-keepy (gate-keepish?) to not lend a hand. *Nice women put others first,* ya' know.

It wouldn't have been *nice* to tell her to stop poaching my content and my customers. Wouldn't have been *nice* to confront her and set a boundary. Wouldn't have been *nice* to respond publicly, rightfully putting her in her place for playing dirty pool. So, I was *nice* instead. I chose to be a nice, compliant, unassuming little woman, ready to make my needs and feelings small for the sake of someone else.

Being nice is centered in politeness. It is about putting others' needs above our own for the sake of being pleasant or pleasing. And, if I'm being honest with myself, it usually has more to do with being perceived a certain way than it does with being honest and authentic.

Kindness is different. Kindness, I've learned, can only be born from authenticity. We are kind when we show up as our true selves. When we are being true to ourselves, we consider other people's needs from a place of empathy *and* self-compassion. We are able to assess their needs in relation to our own, understanding how much we have to give to them while still having enough for ourselves.

Kindness is different. Kindness, I've learned, can only be born from authenticity. We are kind when we show up as our true selves. When we are being true to ourselves, we consider other people's needs from a place of empathy *and* self-compassion.

We do what we can, within reason, to help others. Our helpfulness has limits. We make sure we have steady footing on the mountain before we reach back to help someone else, and we use discernment when choosing whom we reach for. Being kind to others starts with kindness toward ourselves. It means being strategic with our helpfulness so that our good intentions are not taken advantage of or used against us.

Being kind to others starts with kindness toward ourselves. It means being strategic with our helpfulness so that our good intentions are not taken advantage of or used against us.

Self-care is an essential part of being kind. Understanding where limits need to be set for our own well-being—mentally, physically, emotionally, or financially—we can establish healthy boundaries while serving those around us with authenticity and care. Self-care is shrugging off the unfair expectation that women are supposed to be *nice and helpful at all costs.* It is embracing the same shrewdness that men seem so comfortable using in the workplace, recognizing that we are allowed to set limits and look out for our own best interest, too.

Self-care, sprouting from kindness and authenticity, allows us to help others without martyring ourselves at the altar of *nice.* It allows us to take pride in our ability to help others without having regrets. I definitely regret the choices I made with that woman who took advantage of my help. Obviously, if I could do it all again, I'd make different choices. That said, I'd always prefer to be regretfully *nice* than deliberately unkind. What she did, the way she chose to treat me, was unkind at best, sinister at worst, but the world does have a way of sorting people like that out.

Sometimes, self-care is choosing kindness to ourselves over niceness to others and letting karmic justice handle the rest.

Cultivate Your Truth Trench

- **You don't have to be nice to be kind.** Niceness often prioritizes politeness and pleasing others at the expense of your own well-being while kindness stems from authenticity, empathy, and self-compassion. It is good to be kind when you can, but niceness is not something you owe anybody—especially if it means putting your own needs in the back seat.
- **Your time and energy are a limited resource; share them wisely.** Be strategic in offering help and support to others, considering your own needs and limitations before extending assistance. Use discernment when deciding for whom to open doors, with whom to share your network, and to whom to give your precious time and energy.
- **Shrewdness is feminine; protecting your peace is self-care.** Challenge the societal expectation that women must always be nice and accommodating. You are allowed to embrace the same shrewdness and self-interest that men often utilize in professional settings.
- **Setting limits is sensible and kind.** Prioritize kindness to yourself by setting limits, establishing boundaries, and refusing to martyr yourself for the sake of others' expectations or demands, recognizing that self-care is what enables you to be kind to others.

Chapter Twenty-Seven

No More Sports Metaphors

I sometimes wonder when my emails started looking like they were written by a corporate schmo instead of a sparkly woman with enthusiastic, if chaotic, energy.

Maybe it began in graduate school? That seems to make the most sense. I just know that at some point, my emails began losing all their *Amberness.* I used to love using exciting salutations like *G'morning to ya!* And *Why, hello there!* I filled my emails with exclamation marks and emojis, trying my best to bring joy (in a professional way, of course) in every email I sent.

With time, the exclamation marks were replaced with boring old periods. Because, you know, exclamation marks are unprofesh. I was told that emojis made me look like a ditz even though I was often the most educated person on the email chain. I stopped ending my emails with things like "looking forward to hearing back from you!" and changed my farewell to "Best, Amber."

I was taught not to apologize, *ever,* even if I sincerely felt that I was in the wrong. I was told that it makes me look weak and ineffectual. Instead of saying, "I'm sorry for being late," I should say, "Thank you for waiting." I stopped using qualifiers like *I think, does that make sense?* and *maybe I'm wrong, but . . .* and instead just plowed ahead with my thoughts like the men do.

I started using sports metaphors. *The ball's in their court. I'll take a mulligan. Let's throw a Hail Mary. This proposal is a hole-in-one.* Honestly, I didn't understand what half of them meant. Lest you think I'm leaning into sexist tropes here, I know that plenty of women love golf and football and comprehend these terms completely. But that's not me. I learned what a mulligan in golf is because of how it came up in business conversations—it must mean a do-over? Same with a Hail Mary. If we were losing a client and didn't have any moves left, and we did something frantic and sensational instead, that was a Hail Mary. I'm assuming it means something similar in football. I didn't know what I was saying. I just knew that the men seemed to understand. I was successfully assimilating.

But I felt so sad.

In my effort to be taken seriously in workplaces that lean almost exclusively into the male experience, I completely erased what made me, *me*. Employers through the years had told me that exclamation marks and enthusiasm and cheery dispositions are unprofessional. The quiet part, which they never dared to say out loud, was that *my femininity* was unprofessional.

In my effort to be taken seriously in workplaces that lean almost exclusively into the male experience, I completely erased what made me, *me*.

Not every woman experiences her femininity the same. For me, my feminine nature reveals itself though exuberance, passion. My feminine side is quick to apologize when I mess up, and I count that as a strength. My femininity is hot pink lipstick and dramatically winged eyeliner.

It is gentle, understanding, and compassionate, able to diffuse tensions and unify clashing personalities. All of these things I consider strengths, useful qualities that I bring to my colleagues.

Quietly, subversively, the men I worked with taught me that those feminine qualities of mine were weak, not strong. They were defects that needed to be trained out of me, and because I wanted to be successful, acceptable, *pleasing*, I complied.

Hear me, my intrepid friends. There is nothing weak about being feminine, and we do not need to force down our essential selves in order to be "more professional" or "more palatable" in a system that wasn't built with us in mind. I am *so goddamn tired* of this viral trend of women "writing like a man" for a week and celebrating how well it worked. Enough! That is not self-loving, not self-caring, and not liberating to us at all. In fact, it is oppressive. It's squishing our sparkly selves into a box three sizes too small and bragging about how well we fit. It's performing tricks for potato chips from our male colleagues and declaring ourselves full.

Hear me, my intrepid friends. There is nothing weak about being feminine, and we do not need to force down our essential selves in order to be "more professional" or "more palatable" in a system that wasn't built with us in mind.

I'll *never* feel full on the pitiful self-care potato chips of performing for men. What fills me up and nourishes my soul is the difficult self-care of showing up in the workplace exactly as I am. An excitable, animated, glittering, and vivacious spirit who knows the value she brings. So, these days, I wear my hot pink ballet flats to meetings. I say *I'm sorry* when I mean it. I shout and jump for joy, spreading high fives around the room when I feel happy. I use exclamation marks, damn it! And yeah, I swear, too. Swearing is feminine.

This kind of authenticity blossoms outward. It holds the door open for other women to be authentic, too. When my literary agent gave me the call to offer representation for this book, we shrieked, and yelled, and celebrated. I fell to my knees, letting her hear the exhilaration in my voice, not swallowing the lump in my throat but letting it spill out in sobs. She brought all her divine, sparkling, feminine, and strong energy to the call, too.

There we were, two fierce women, embracing ourselves exactly the way we are. No pretense. No veneer of the "professionalism" that men like to train us into. Just two women. Celebrating the joy, and the thrill, and the hope of mutual success. Exactly as we are. Authentically.

Real self-care is women showing up in their feminine power.

Together. Real. Strong.

And sparkly.

Cultivate Your Truth Trench

- **Feminine authenticity and expression are divine.** Celebrate feminine expression in all its forms, whether it's through exuberance, creativity, or passion, recognizing that authenticity and diversity enrich the workplace and contribute to collective success.
- **Masculinity should not be the default.** There is societal pressure to behave like men in the workplace, which sometimes means leaning into the masculine side of our nature instead of the feminine one. This is because femininity is *still* thought of by some as weaker than masculinity. Feminine qualities such as enthusiasm, compassion, and empathy are strengths that can enhance workplace dynamics and contribute to success rather than weaknesses to be suppressed or trained out.
- **You're allowed to sparkle.** Prioritize self-care by refusing to compromise your authenticity and femininity for the sake of fitting into traditional workplace norms. Instead, nurture your spirit by showing up as your true self.
- **Self-care blossoms outward.** Lead by example by creating a supportive environment where women feel empowered to embrace their authentic selves without fear of judgment or reprisal, fostering a culture of inclusivity and acceptance. Support other women in their journey to embrace their feminine power and authenticity, amplifying one another's voices and experiences to create a stronger, more inclusive workplace culture.

Chapter Twenty-Eight

Profits

I've spent a lot of time mentoring women who want to start their own business. I *love* having these conversations—hearing their dreams, their plans. I've met so many brave and highly capable women through that work, but there is one thing that has come up in almost every single one of those conversations. I have lost count of how many of these women have told me, "I don't even want to make money; I just have a cool concept and I want to share it with the world."

This is an almost exclusively female idea. Society tells us that our contributions are meant to be for the greater good. We are instructed to be charitable, to teach, to give comfort. All the adjectives used to describe women engender a feeling of softness, of selflessness. Of course it's okay for us to want to earn money for our labor, but there are *limits, don't you know.* The world is okay with us making enough money to provide for our children, to comfort our husbands, to help with the bills if possible. But dare a woman say that she wants to be wealthy? To live in luxury? To profit from the game of capitalism that was intended to only benefit men? That, my dear, is too far. *Too far.*

This is the moral imperative of selflessness that patriarchy has placed on women. For centuries, society has labeled selflessness for the collective good as a decidedly feminine virtue. Patriarchy says that when we pursue "selfish" things that do not serve the collective good, we are violating some innate part of our nature. How are we supposed to tend to our physical, mental, emotional, and professional well-being when we are told any steps we take toward *self* are *selfish?*

Men are blissfully unburdened by these kinds of labels. While women are called selfish or aggressive for wanting financial prosperity, men with the same traits are applauded for their ambition, drive, and entrepreneurial spirit. This double standard often stops women from pursuing their financial goals, and they decide that it is better to make less money for their labor than to be called greedy and selfish.

Not that I'm telling you anything new here, but the other problem we tend to face is society's idea that because we are women, we must (a) be married, (b) have children, and therefore (c) focus primarily on our families' needs over our careers. When we prioritize our career goals and financial success, we are told that we are neglecting our innate duties of wife, mother, and caretaker. They ask us:

Who is taking care of your kids while you're here at work?

You shouldn't have had kids if you weren't ready to sacrifice your dreams.

How does your husband feel about you caring more about your career than your children?

Of course, men aren't held under that kind of scrutiny. They are free to pursue their dreams, their notoriety, their achievements, and their financial success. As we all know, this horrible disparity only serves to further marginalize and subjugate women.

The long-term work of self-care for women in the workplace is stepping into our power in business and industry. It is outrageous that we should be less interested in success and prosperity just because we are women. Being humble and self-sacrificing is not *in our nature.* It is not *how we were born.* That is how we were raised, how we were indoctrinated. We believe these things to be true because the world has told us they are true.

Women who know how to pursue their dreams, their careers, and yes, their financial success are a threat. They challenge unfair gender roles that men have profited from for centuries. They cannot be held underfoot by insecure husbands who want them financially dependent. They won't be silent when they are overlooked and underpaid for opportunities they would be qualified for, if only they had a well-groomed beard and a Y chromosome.

Women who know how to pursue their dreams, their careers, and yes, their financial success are a threat. They challenge unfair gender roles that men have profited from for centuries.

Women who know how to pursue their dreams won't settle for *less than* just because someone told them they should.

My long journey of self-care in the workplace has meant embracing my desire for financial success and prosperity, speaking openly about it, and sharing my zest for turning a profit. It has come with plenty of criticism.

My first time being criticized for making steps toward financial prosperity happened when I launched my line of luxury leather diaper bags, purses, and accessories. There were many women who chastened me for my prices—they were too expensive, too exclusionary—but I had done my research. I knew that I had the highest quality leather and materials, that the factory I was using was top-notch. I also knew that similar bags, of similar quality, could be found in literally any department store in the United States for equal to double that price. Most importantly, I knew my costs.

I priced my bags in a way that all my expenses—cost of materials, cost of labor, quality control assessments, international shipping, import fees, and more—were covered by the retail price of the bag *and* that allowed me to make a profit. It wasn't an outrageous profit, but it was substantial. From those profits, I paid my employees (all of them female). I bought them iPads. I gave them bonuses, paid for their travel. I enriched their lives in every way I knew how. I quietly used those profits to help members of my community who were in need. I donated to nonprofits for women. I invested in small women-owned and black-owned businesses in my community for my warehouse needs instead of big box retailers like Staples.

And!

I took care of myself and my family.

I am not ashamed of that.

In fact, I'm pretty goddamn proud.

That is self-care: choosing to not be ashamed of working hard and earning a profit; not being ashamed of engaging with profits the way a man does, unapologetically; not giving anyone an explanation for why I deserve to profit from my work; being *incredibly proud* of what I've done and pricing my labor accordingly; using my profits to uplift women and make their lives better so that they, in turn, can uplift other women.

This is how we take back power. It is how we create a redistribution of wealth and influence that *actually* serves

This is how we take back power. It is how we create a redistribution of wealth and influence that *actually* serves the greater good.

the greater good. Ironic, now that I think about it, how when we embrace our perfectly natural desire for success and wealth, those things naturally flow to the people around us. We can be charitable *because* we insisted on earning what we are worth. We can help other women *because* we decide not to sell ourselves short.

We can't sustain ourselves on the last crumbly bits of potato chips at the bottom of the bag. We shouldn't be expected to. If we hope to do any real good in the world, we can't be starving ourselves. In order to feed ourselves and do the good work we want to do, we must prepare a feast, a feast for ourselves that we share with others from our abundance.

Cultivate Your Truth Trench

- **Pursue prosperity like a man.** Embrace the desire for financial success and prosperity unapologetically, understanding that it is not selfish but rather empowering to strive for economic independence and security, regardless of gender.
- **There is value in everything you touch, create, or inspire.** Recognize and affirm your own worth and the value of your labor. You shouldn't have to settle for less than what you deserve. Price your work accordingly without the need for justification or apology.
- **It isn't *prideful* to be proud.** Reject some people's idea that women who are proud of their work, accomplishments, or creations are prideful. You deserve to be proud of the work you've done, and you do not need to be small about it.
- **Prosperity enables you to empower other women.** Financial success allows you to uplift not only yourself but also others in the community by using profits to support and empower women-owned businesses, contribute to charitable causes, and provide opportunities for economic advancement.

Chapter Twenty-Nine

Baby-Wearing Businesswoman

It was, at the time, the biggest moment yet for me and my small business.

I had finally secured a meeting with one of the top retail brands in the baby industry, and I was going to ask to become one of their only online retailers. Brands in the baby market tend not to work with online retailers, preferring to work exclusively with businesses who have a brick-and-mortar store, but I just knew I could convince them to make an exception if I could get in their ear.

This was my shot.

I found out just a few minutes prior to my Zoom meeting that Charlie was going to have to go to the office unexpectedly, leaving me alone with our then nine-month-old baby. I thought about asking to postpone the meeting. I knew my baby well enough by that time to know that he was absolutely not going to cooperate for me while I took this very important call. But you don't risk canceling a meeting you worked so hard to get for fear that you'll never get back on their calendar. So, I decided to roll with it.

I pulled out my trusty baby carrier, put my son in the front-carry position with his chest pressed against mine, and joined the Zoom call. Honestly, things went pretty well—at first. Aside from yanking my hair and eliciting a shriek out of me a few times, my baby was mostly tame. We were making progress with negotiations; we were just about to finalize the deal.

And that was the exact moment that my son decided to puke directly into my cleavage.

I had a breastfeeding tank on, which had a low neckline. My skin was obscured by my baby's head so that the folks on the call couldn't see anything, but that didn't stop the searing humiliation of feeling fresh baby puke slowly seep between my breasts. It also didn't help matters that, after puking down my shirt, he pulled a move straight from *The Exorcist*, spinning his head unnaturally around to face the camera and projectile vomiting toward everyone on the call. Mortified, I did the only thing I knew to do in that moment. I apologized and hung up.

Didn't even try to schedule a follow-up meeting.

I eventually recovered from the humiliation, and as the years went on, I took hundreds more phone calls wearing babies. I loved the privilege of being able to work from home or anywhere I wanted without being away from my little ones, but I couldn't help the crushing overwhelm of stress these baby-wearing phone calls gave me. I usually ended up with pit stains and a headache before they were over.

It wasn't just the fear of something embarrassing happening during the call. I learned how to recover with grace from those unexpected mishaps. What actually brought me down, what put an ache in my heart, was the constant worry that I'd never be taken seriously as a businesswoman. Was it even fair to expect people to take me seriously when I showed up to meetings wearing a cartoon-covered baby carrier and my hair on day three of a messier-by-the-day messy bun? I was so hungry to be successful, to be seen as a shrewd and formidable entrepreneur. Instead, I looked like an exhausted, puke-covered zombie. I felt worthless and small. I felt unqualified and concluded that everyone else saw me that way, too.

This is a uniquely female experience. No matter how hard men try to sympathize, most will never understand. I remember, back in those years with little ones, listening to Charlie tell me about the stress of his job when he came home in the evenings. To me, it all sounded wonderful. Sitting in air-conditioned conference rooms discussing *boring* adult stuff instead of making hundreds of trips to the pantry for toddler snacks while watching the same episode of *Blippi* for the seventh time in a row. Attending *exhausting* corporate lunches where the wine is flowing and someone brings your food to you rather than you serving your two demanding children with bottomless stomachs. Having *the pressure* of huge projects because you are known as the most capable person on the team, instead of slowly losing your identity and becoming more invisible with every passing day.

I knew his work was hard, and it wasn't fair of me to compare. Still. His privilege was that every difficult situation at his job wasn't made more difficult by having to quiet cranky babies and rowdy toddlers while trying not to have a whole-ass mental breakdown in front of his coworkers and clients.

I just don't believe that this is an experience that the majority of men can

I just don't believe that this is an experience that the majority of men can understand. They are applauded for their diligent devotion to their work, even if they neglect or ignore their families once they get home, even if they do nothing to ease the 24/7 burden of domestic labor that their wives shoulder alone.

understand. They are applauded for their diligent devotion to their work, even if they neglect or ignore their families once they get home, even if they do nothing to ease the 24/7 burden of domestic labor that their wives shoulder alone. If they do contribute even the very barest of the bare minimum, they are met with delighted praise for being *such supportive partners*! They exist in a world in which working at all is considered a sacrifice for their families, and if they offer even an iota of help around the house, they are heroes.

When we, on the other hand, attempt to have a career and a family at the same time, we are criticized, belittled. We are seen as unreliable employees when we have to leave work to pick up a sick kid from school (a task that our husbands simply couldn't be expected to do). We are called selfish mothers when we hand our kids their tablets so that we can meet a deadline. We are exhausted, overwhelmed, and unappreciated at work and at home. We try to balance family and career the same way that men do, but often end up feeling like failures at both.

This struggle between career and family has been an excellent sandbox for learning to set boundaries and limits around both how I spend my time and what expectations I allow other people to put on me.

This struggle between career and family has been an excellent sandbox for learning to set boundaries and limits around both how I spend my time and what expectations I allow other people to put on me. This difficult work of self-care has meant becoming my own human resources department, in my work and in my home. I sometimes even imagine myself in a tailored suit and sensible heels when I do this work. Something about envisioning myself as a polished HR rep makes me feel emboldened to advocate for myself, even if I'm actually on day five of working in the same pair of black leggings.

Whether you work in a traditional workplace or are self-employed, there are boundaries and expectations you can set for yourself to preserve your dignity, sanity, and personhood. A personal expectation I chose to set for myself was to accept that maybe my two-year plan will need to look more like a five-year plan. I chose to understand that being a mom *will* impact the speed with which I can achieve my career goals. Managing that expectation has kept a lot of disappointment and frustration at bay. I've also become really up-front with employees, clients, and customers about my lifestyle. I am on point with my kids, always. If they need me, I have to put them first. That means that there are some career opportunities that are just not for me.

Eventually, my hope is that all workplaces will accommodate their employees' family responsibilities (more on that in the next chapter). For now, we have to figure out how to advocate for ourselves in workplaces that might not advocate for us.

We also have to advocate for ourselves in our own homes when it comes to our work. I've had to learn the difficult skill of setting (and upholding) boundaries with my children, especially when they are home from school for summer or holidays. I've learned to say things like "my work doesn't stop just because you don't have school," and "I can't be your playmate today, you'll have to keep yourself busy." I've had to insist, as we discussed at the beginning of this book, that my husband shares equitably in the household labor with me. I've had to learn that I can't keep the house

I've learned to say things like "my work doesn't stop just because you don't have school," and "I can't be your playmate today, you'll have to keep yourself busy."

immaculately clean, cook gourmet meals, make my home look like a living Pinterest board, and keep my body perfectly tanned and toned while also keeping my career alive. I've accepted that sometimes Ramen noodles and Goldfish are perfectly acceptable dinner foods, both for the kids and for us. I've also become well acquainted with the Tackl app, where I can delegate work *or* home tasks (when possible) to someone else to buy back some of my time.

A lot has changed now that my kids are older. It's easier now, but I'll never forget the days of puke rolling sickeningly down my cleavage while I smiled through an important meeting. If those are the times you're living in, mama, you aren't alone. I promise it gets better, gets easier. Wherever you find yourself in the career-woman to juggling-job-and-kids pipeline, please start the work of professional self-care right now. Until the world accepts that the experience of working moms is fundamentally different from the experience of working dads, we have to be the ones to set boundaries and expectations—both for ourselves and for others.

Until the world accepts that the experience of working moms is fundamentally different from the experience of working dads, we have to be the ones to set boundaries and expectations.

Like all kinds of self-care, the work is hard but worth it.

Cultivate Your Truth Trench

- **Sensible self-care means setting realistic expectations of yourself.** Managing expectations around career goals and family responsibilities can help you avoid becoming discouraged and frustrated. Things may take more time than you think when balancing work with maternal obligations. Adjust your expectations to create a more realistic and sustainable approach to achieving success.
- **You require and deserve support.** Give yourself permission to advocate for your needs in the workplace and at home. There is nothing shameful in utilizing available resources and support systems, such as childcare assistance, task delegation apps, and equitable distribution of household labor with your partner, to alleviate stress and create space for personal and professional growth.
- **Set boundaries and speak your needs.** Communicate openly about personal boundaries and lifestyle priorities, asserting the need for flexibility and understanding as you manage competing demands.
- **Seek progress, not perfection.** Celebrate progress and resilience in navigating the challenges of balancing career aspirations with family responsibilities, recognizing that each step toward self-care and boundary setting at work and at home is a valuable achievement.

Chapter Thirty

The Assignment

How different would the world look if women were stepping into their power, starting businesses with our needs in mind, and sucking the female talent out of male-dominated spaces? What if we skipped the #instablessed MLM schemes that pretend to uplift women but actually prey on them and sunk our teeth instead into the work of *actually* empowering women?

My apologies to the MLM babes, but I do have to talk about the problem of multilevel marketing for a moment. I need to talk about how businesses like these (MLMs, Ponzi schemes, pyramid schemes, etc.) have the veneer of empowering women but actually crush them further underfoot. I need you to understand that I'm not criticizing you. I'm challenging the predatory nature of these types of businesses who suck in and spit out sparkly women like you. It'll be quick and relatively painless, but we do need to talk about it.

MLMs are the potato chips of women's empowerment in the workplace. In fact, they're the *Spicy Cajun Crawtaters* of potato chips. We really could do without them, and yet, they exist.

Let's start with the fact that almost every MLM organization you've heard of was either founded, or is currently led, by men: Beach

Body (Carl Daikeler, founder), Mary Kay (Ryan Rogers, CEO), Arbonne (Tyler Whitehead, CEO), Younique (Derek Maxfield, CEO), MONAT (Ray & Luis Urdaneta, Founders), and LulaRoe (Mark Stidham & DeAnne Brady, Founders), just to name a few.

It's not hard to spot the soft misogyny in these organizations—the "we understand women to the extent that we still see their primary purpose as being wives and mothers" way in which they approach their business. They promise women quick and easy money all while working from anywhere with flexible schedules (primarily so that they can focus on their husbands and kids). They capitalize on the hopes and dreams of often vulnerable women by promising unrealistic outcomes that only the top 1 percent of the pyramid actually sees. They coach women to call themselves CEOs and small business owners without teaching them any of the qualities or skills needed to do what real CEOs and small business owners do every day. (If that ruffles your feathers, I'd gently ask, have you as an MLM business owner ever had to plan quarterly product releases, manage employee paychecks, hire and fire people, handle HR and PR crises, pay exorbitant import fees to get your merchandise stateside, or provide tax forms to employees?) To make the point even clearer, when the Amazon Prime documentary *LuLaRich* was released in 2021, we learned that although many of these organizations position women as the face and social media voice of the business, they coach those women to let their husbands make the big decisions—you know, the CEO-type stuff—all while parading women around as the "self-made CEOs" of their business.

This stuff is paternalistic at best and misogynistic at worst. It still positions women as dainty little homemakers whose career ambitions matter to the extent that they "help support the family."

This stuff is paternalistic at best and misogynistic at worst. It still positions women as dainty little homemakers whose career ambitions matter to the extent that they "help support the family." It does nothing to truly equip women to achieve big goals and real success. And sadly, the data shows us that most of the women who invest in these MLM schemes end up losing most of their investment and having nothing to show for all their hard work and sacrifice.

When I started The Sensible Mama and LYMIA BRAND, I decided that my main goal was going to be hiring women, prioritizing their needs, and creating an environment that they would want to stay in. I also wanted to make sure that if they left the company for any reason, they would have a really incredible job title and description to put on their résumé. I was a first-time CEO. I knew I would make mistakes, and I did. But I knew I had to try, had to give it my all. My heart was in the right place and that would hopefully counteract my lack of experience.

I had a very small staff. That gave me some agility, the freedom to experiment. I figured I could establish the culture I wanted for my business in these early stages so that it could be cultivated and maintained as we grew.

I started by allowing employees who could do their jobs from home to do that whenever they needed. No questions asked—just a heads-up required. For employees whose jobs couldn't be done from home, I gave them permission to bring their kids to work when necessary.

Yes, this did lead to some awkward moments. Once, we accidentally shipped one of our kid's bouncy balls with an order. Another time, a Ziplock bag of another kid's Cheerios was found in someone's delivery. I understood that some people would call that unprofessional, but because I had loudly professed myself as a business that employs and supports moms in the workplace, I hoped that customers would understand. And they did! They found it endearing, and soon enough it was a coveted surprise to receive an "extra gift from The Sensible Mama babies" in your order.

I had an understanding with my employees that as long as their work got done, I didn't care when or how they got it done. I often had employees doing their jobs from pediatricians' waiting rooms, on bleachers at soccer games, or while sitting in car line. There were periods during the day when I expected remote employees to be available to take phone calls or have staff meetings, but even those were flexible if an unforeseen situation with the kids came up.

It was important to me that my business was a safe haven for moms who were accustomed to being treated like a burden in the workplace. And look, I get it. I know that child-free people often feel frustrated and discouraged when they have to pick up slack for parents who have to duck out to deal with kid-related things. To those of you who are here, I want you to know that you deserve the same family accommodations that parents get. I'm sorry it sometimes feels like parents have an irrefutable excuse to leave work, but your reasons are often ignored or invalidated. That's not right.

In my case, everyone who worked for me was a mom. So, we decided that our team culture would be one of *mutual regard*. We looked out for one another. We didn't keep score. If someone had to take the day off with a sick kid, someone else stepped up to take care of their responsibilities. They understood that when it was their turn to need help, someone would step up for them, too.

When I opened my 4,000 square foot warehouse, the first thing we did was knock down a wall between two adjoining offices and turn that space into a playroom for kids who came to work with us.

When all our kids were finally at school age and we no longer needed a place for them to play, I turned the playroom into a gym. It was embarrassingly underequipped. But! It had a treadmill, free weights, a barbell, a yoga mat, and a television. Gym memberships are expensive, and who really has guilt-free time to get there anyway? If my employees got a chance to take care of their bodies (or blow off some steam) during their work hours where no one could guilt or interrupt them, that was fine by me.

The bathroom stayed stocked with feminine products and a few hairstyling products as well. I did my best to keep the kitchen stocked with essentials, paid for by the business: water, coffee, sodas, and lots of snacks. It was meager, but it was something. We had breastfeeding women on staff, and they needed to stay nourished and hydrated.

Employees had mental health days, just like sick days, that they could take at any time with absolutely no questions asked. They got bonuses when we had product launches and big sales, free and heavily discounted products, and compensation that was at the top end of what would be expected for their job title. They needed to be able to live.

Perhaps the thing I'm most proud of was how their job titles were handled. Everyone who worked for me was given a very impressive job title, and they usually got to provide input on what their title should be. We used titles like *Director of Customer Experience, Warehouse Logistics Manager,* and *Senior Director of Social Media Marketing* instead of Customer Service Rep, Stocker/Shipper, or Community Manager. This was easy to do as a small business. I'm sure it would be a challenge with a bigger organization, but I had an opportunity to give my small staff a really great sounding title for their resumé, so why not?

These small things have a way of rippling outward, turning a small current into a tidal wave. They change women's lives. They put success and happiness within reach. They empower women to succeed, not just in their current job, but in their future jobs as well.

These were small things, easy things, things that any business owner could do to make the workplace more accessible and rewarding to women and moms. These small things have a way of rippling outward, turning a small current into a tidal wave. They change women's lives. They put success and happiness within reach. They empower women to succeed, not just in their current job, but in their future jobs as well. And yes, they make home life easier, too. They enable women to cultivate a life that makes room for self-care and for the care of their loved ones.

Women, this work is doable. We can commit to creating these spaces, and we must. I will never stop thinking of my daughter and what kind of workplace I am leaving behind for her. I don't know what she's going to be like as an adult. I try my best to teach her about boldness and assertiveness—being loud and taking up space—but so far, at her tender age, it seems like my daughter might possess a gentle spirit, one that might not be as comfortable standing up for herself and others as I have become. For the future of our gentle daughters, it's time that we start advocating for these changes now. And for our more fiery daughters, it's time that we forge an example for them to follow. Self-care is making sure that every space we stand in, including the corporate space, accommodates our needs. We can forge those spaces out of what already exists, or we can create them ourselves.

For the future of our gentle daughters, it's time that we start advocating for these changes now. And for our more fiery daughters, it's time that we forge an example for them to follow.

Cultivate Your Truth Trench

- **Women deserve career spaces that consider our needs.** If you are someone who has power in the workplace, prioritize hiring women and creating supportive environments where women's needs are accommodated and opportunities for growth and advancement are cultivated.
- **Be the advocate that you and other women deserve.** When possible, advocate for workplaces that provide resources and amenities that support women's physical and mental well-being, including mental health days and childcare facilities.
- **Use your influence to prepare women for better futures.** One way for female employers to equip their female employees for bright futures is to give them impressive job titles that reflect their contributions and accomplishments, empowering them to take pride in their roles and enhancing their professional profiles for future career opportunities.
- **Our choices today impact the women of tomorrow.** Commit to making the workplace more accessible and rewarding for women by implementing small, impactful changes that ripple outward, fostering success, happiness, and self-care for female employees. These small changes will lead to positive systemic change for our future generations of women.

SECTION V

Comfort Food:

Self-Care in Our Mental Health

Chapter Thirty-One

Little-t Trauma

If diving into trauma in the very first chapter on mental health feels a bit jarring to you, don't worry, it feels like that to me, too. It's weird. We all bristle a little at the word *trauma*. It makes us uncomfortable. But I need to start here. I have to because if I don't, I fear you will not realize that this entire section of the book is for you.

A lot of us women (hi, hello, it's me) have a really annoying way of minimizing our pain. We compare our circumstances to other people's and decide that ours aren't that bad. They're probably not worth complaining about, much less *doing* anything about.

When we think about trauma, we usually think of things like going to war or enduring profound abuse, neglect, or grief. These are called the "Big-T traumas." They are the big, universal traumas that anyone on earth would hear about and say, *Oh, yeah, that definitely sucks*. Most of us agree that Big-T traumas require lots of healing, therapy, and self-care to overcome. What we, *especially* we women, fail to understand is that our "little-t" traumas are just as important to heal and recover from.

Little-t traumas are overwhelming experiences that can have long-lasting negative effects but that aren't widely accepted as *trauma* the way that Big-T traumas are. These are things like changing jobs, divorce, relocating, infidelity, financial struggles, friendship breakups, the death of a pet, or interpersonal conflict. I guess a better way to say it is that little-t trauma is anything that causes you emotional turmoil, and it is defined solely by you. *Anything* can be a little-t trauma.

Little-t trauma is *anything* that causes you emotional turmoil and it is defined solely by you. Anything can be a little-t trauma.

Why am I belaboring this point? Because, my friend, I suspect that you have a list of your own little-t traumas that you've been brushing under the metaphorical rug for a while now.

It's time to let them out.

Having unresolved little-t traumas can show up in the way you engage with the world. Sometimes, these traumas cause you to act in ways you feel ashamed of. For example, I have some little-t traumas from the early years of my marriage that I'm still working through in therapy. I've mostly got them under control, but every now and then one of those little-t traumas gets activated. It's usually my husband who accidentally steps on those land mines because he's the one who put them there. When that happens, I lash out instantly before I've even let myself process what he *actually* said or did. In that moment, I'm living in our old marriage. I get angsty and irritable. I can't be reasoned with. I storm off. Later, I fuss at my kids for doing normal kid stuff because *I* am so dysregulated. I change the temperature of our entire household because a Tic Tac–sized problem triggered me into asteroid-sized dysfunction.

I am ashamed when I act that way. When I finally pull myself together, I have to apologize to everyone. Ask for their forgiveness. Promise to do better.

They deserve for me to do better. Those little-t traumas happened years ago. My family deserves for me to love myself and them enough to acknowledge that the pain is still there and to do something to fix it. That's why I stay in therapy, even though I am in a much healthier place than I was when I started.

Is there a little-t trauma in your life that you've been tucking away, out of sight, out of mind? Is it bubbling up in strange and confusing ways that you have to apologize for later? If so, I urge you to read on with the understanding that what follows is for you. You don't need to discount, minimize, or disqualify your own pain just because it may not seem as big as someone else's.

> **You don't need to discount, minimize, or disqualify your own pain just because it may not seem as big as someone else's.**

As women, we've been conditioned to make ourselves small, often denying the validity of our own struggles in comparison to those who've experienced "real" trauma. But here's the truth: Taking care of our mental health by confronting and healing from our own pain is one of the most important forms of self-care we can undertake. And we can't do that until we acknowledge, deeply and fully, that our pain matters.

It matters tremendously.

It matters spectacularly.

There is no pain too small to deserve to be healed.

Cultivate Your Truth Trench

- **Your little-t traumas are valid.** Acknowledge the significance of little-t traumas, which may not be widely recognized but can have long-lasting negative effects on mental health. Little-t traumas can be anything, but they usually include experiences like job changes, divorce, financial struggles, and interpersonal conflicts, and every one of them matters.
- **Your pain doesn't need to be compared to anyone else's.** Your pain and struggles, no matter how small or insignificant they seem compared to others,' are valid and deserving of acknowledgment and healing. Challenge the tendency to minimize or discount your own experiences because "someone else had it worse."
- **Unhealed pain will impact your relationships if you do nothing about it.** Unresolved little-t traumas can manifest in behavior patterns that cause shame and regret, affecting relationships and daily functioning, even years later. If left unaddressed, they can prompt actions or reactions that feel out of control or disproportionate to the situation. You deserve to heal and to have healthy, sustainable relationships.
- **It is brave to acknowledge your pain and commit to healing.** The first step toward healing your pain is to admit that it's there and that the brave act of self-care takes real courage and real work. Embrace the importance of seeking therapy and engaging in self-care practices to address and heal from little-t traumas, and acknowledge that ongoing efforts are necessary even as progress is made.

Chapter Thirty-Two

Daily Dose of SSRI

I was stagnating in therapy.

It had been two years. My therapist and I had unpacked and reprocessed every painful memory from childhood to adulthood, and I still felt unfixed. We had worked through my Big-T traumas, but there were still lots of little-t land mines I kept stepping in. We tried EMDR therapy, Parts Work therapy, attachment therapy. It felt like my therapist had emptied out his entire bag of tricks, and I didn't feel any better.

Charlie and I were still separated. I had done so much work on myself but still couldn't decide if I wanted to divorce or reconcile. I was living in this purgatory nightmare where I couldn't move forward or back. I was stuck.

Cataclysmically stuck.

One day, Charlie came to my apartment to talk. He wanted to know if I was any closer to making my decision about our marriage. I got angry and defensive—mad that he was pushing me when I wasn't ready, mad that I couldn't be ready even if I tried. I felt naked and exposed. Charlie asked me how therapy was going, and I told him how stuck I was. Gently, he asked if I would consider talking to my therapist about getting on a selective serotonin reuptake inhibitor (otherwise known as an SSRI or, more commonly, an antidepressant). He knew my history with severe anxiety, and there were some signs that I was also depressed. "Maybe if you'd just take something to help your mind process things, you'd unstuck yourself," he'd said.

I took exception to this idea. I mentioned earlier that my mom had a complicated relationship with her mental health, and it seemed to me that she had a very low opinion of mental health medications. Or maybe she had a low opinion of herself for needing them. I internalized some of that and found myself feeling offended by the suggestion that I might need them, too. But I was at least able to understand that I had expired every other option and didn't have anything to lose by trying. I told Charlie that I would talk to my therapist. If getting on the SSRI didn't give me any clarity as to whether he and I should reconcile or divorce, I was going to file for divorce. I at least had to release Charlie from the limbo I was putting us in with my indecision.

My therapist was on board. He agreed that maybe we had done all we could do with therapy alone and that maybe getting on an SSRI would bring me the clarity that I needed to keep processing my feelings.

I saw a specialist and was diagnosed with severe anxiety (which I already knew), as well as mild depression (which managed to catch me by surprise). I was given a prescription for Sertraline, the generic version of Zoloft. The specialist told me that it could take up to six months to see any results, so stay hopeful and persistent. To my surprise, I felt a change in my mood and function within a few short weeks. After around five days of almost debilitating drug-induced exhaustion (I was told that might happen), I emerged from the fog feeling refreshed, clearheaded. It was a small step, but it was something.

With time, there were more changes. One of them was the intensity with which I felt my emotions. I was used to experiencing every emotion at the extreme ends of the spectrum. I was either exuberantly happy or profoundly sad. At all times, I was either a zero or a ten, always on a high or a low. Nothing in between. On the SSRI, I stopped feeling the tens, the breathtaking highs that I always looked forward to. Suddenly, it felt like my happiness was blocked by a glass ceiling. I dearly missed those tens.

The absence of the tens would have sent me into a downward spiral if it hadn't been for the fact that I was *also* not feeling the zeros. I wasn't plummeting to the abyss every time something didn't go my way, and that was exhilarating. It was like the SSRI gave me a safety net; it would only let me fall so far. My emotional range had shifted away from zero to ten, and now existed safely in the three to seven range. I still missed the tens, but it sure was incredible to not feel the zeros.

The absence of the tens would have sent me into a downward spiral if it hadn't been for the fact that I was *also* not feeling the zeros. I wasn't plummeting to the abyss every time something didn't go my way, and that was exhilarating.

It seemed like a fair trade.

Clarity soon came. Unencumbered by the distraction of yo-yoing between the zeros and the tens, I was able to focus on the real work I needed to do in therapy. I felt like a drainpipe that had been all gunked up and that suddenly got un-gunked. Things started to make sense. Little-t traumas began to heal, the scab slowly peeling away and revealing new, undamaged flesh underneath. I saw a clear vision of my future, and that future included Charlie. I felt ready and able to do the hard work we would need to do to make that happen.

And the rest, my friend, is history.

Why am I sharing this story here and not in the chapters about my marriage? I'm glad you asked. I'm sharing this here because it belongs here.

I deserve to be my happiest, fullest, highest self. Why would I deprive myself of the tools that can help me do that?

Getting on an SSRI was not the solution to a marriage problem. It was the solution to a brain anatomy problem, a therapeutic problem, an *Amber not being her very best self* problem. It was, in its truest form, a self-care problem. I am still on my SSRI even though my life is steady and stable now. I will be on it for the foreseeable future—maybe, in some form, for the rest of my life. I am still in therapy, too, and as long as I am able to afford it, even if it's only once every few months, I will continue to go. I deserve to be my happiest, fullest, highest self. Why would I deprive myself of the tools that can help me do that?

Some of us think of therapy, antidepressants, and SSRIs as crutches. Or at least that's what a lot of us were told by our Boomer parents. Yet, we understand that even a skilled rock climber hooks himself to the mountain so that he can climb safely. Even an experienced pilot uses navigation equipment to land the plane. We don't call these things crutches because they *aren't crutches.* They are necessary tools to keep people safe and at their peak performance.

We don't call these things crutches because they *aren't crutches.* They are necessary tools to keep people safe and at their peak performance.

Millennials are more concerned with taking care of their mental health than any generation that came before them. And still, many of us are held prisoner to outdated stigmas that aren't rooted in truth or even in reality. Going to therapy isn't for "babies." Taking antidepressants isn't "something the snowflakes do." You aren't weak or pathetic or a loser for needing therapy or a little brain medicine. In fact, you are admirably strong.

Self-care means being brave enough to seek out the tools you need to be your happiest, healthiest, and wisest self.

Cultivate Your Truth Trench

- **You deserve to chase down every possible avenue of mental health and healing.** Therapy is great, but there are potential limitations of traditional therapy in addressing mental health concerns. There are benefits to exploring pharmaceutical interventions, such as SSRIs, in conjunction with therapy to get the most impact out of your mental health journey.
- **There is no shame in brain science.** Seeking help through medication is a personal journey and not a sign of weakness. Sometimes your brain needs a little help, and self-care is getting it what it needs to help you feel your best. Love yourself enough to find out if medicine might be beneficial for your mental health and well-being. There is no shame in that.
- **It's okay to grieve the changes.** There are emotional shifts that come with taking mental health medications. While you might miss some of the highest highs, you will probably never miss the lowest lows. It's okay to grieve the loss of the highs while acknowledging that it is a worthwhile loss if it means avoiding the lows.
- **Medications can remove roadblocks to healing.** Sometimes, your brain chemistry can only take you so far. When you meet roadblocks in your therapy sessions or healing journey, it may be because you have pushed your brain to its capacity. Taking medications can help you not only feel more regulated but may also help you be more productive in your healing.

Chapter Thirty-Three

Imposter Syndrome

I am not a fraud. I know this, and yet, I don't.

The strange paradox of imposter syndrome is that when others say they like me or believe in me, I don't believe them. But when they find me unlikeable or don't think I can succeed, I do believe them. Which is it? Do I trust these people or don't I?

Imposter syndrome is the persistent belief that anything good or worthy that happens to you is not the result of your own skill, talents, or efforts but is instead the result of coincidence or good fortune. It is also the belief that anything bad that happens to you *is* a result of your own effort or choices. In short, imposter syndrome tells us that anything bad that happens to us is our fault, and anything good that happens isn't. It is a terrible beast, and it preys largely on women. It just seems like men don't struggle with imposter syndrome the way we do. Think about it, when has anyone seen a mediocre man believe he couldn't do absolutely anything he put his mind to, and do it well? Blissfully unburdened by the need to be qualified, informed, or competent, men are free to try their hand at anything they want.

Plenty of capable, kind, and talented women struggle every day with self-doubt, believing that they are not smart enough, good enough, or competent enough to do the things they yearn to do. We gaslight ourselves into believing that we are frauds, charlatans. At work, we hesitate to ask for promotions we deserve because we fear people might discover we are less intelligent than we seem. In our friendships, we question whether we truly belong or if everyone has realized that we're not all that fun or interesting after all. And in our marriages, we wonder if our spouses would still love us if they knew who we *really* are.

I struggle with this almost constantly. In fact, I feel chronically under-qualified in every single aspect of my life. There is this belief deep in my bones that everyone else is smarter than me, kinder, more capable, and it's only a matter of time until everyone realizes it. I recognize that the world seems to respond to me as though I am all of those things—that, indeed, I am a shining example of them. But I spend a *way more than necessary* amount of my time telling myself that if they really knew me, they wouldn't think of me that way.

Maybe it's because I know my internal experiences and they don't. They see me confidently reaching for new opportunities and trying new things. They don't see all the negative self-talk, the self-doubt, the absolute soul-crushing fear I have to shove down first. I do it scared; they think I do it brave.

They see me living publicly and loudly on the internet, sharing my highs and lows with confidence without seeming to care what other people think. They don't see how often I sit in silence, reflecting on the daily criticism I get from strangers on the internet, secretly believing the criticism is true.

They see me hanging out with friends, laughing and having fun. They don't see my nearly debilitating social anxiety, my fears that I'm not a very likable person and that everyone is just putting up with me to be polite. My belief that, one day, I'll be all alone. The bubbly, confident little girl I used to be, who believed she could do anything, has slowly vanished. In her place is an anxious, self-doubting grown-up who wonders if she can do anything at all.

This is exactly how imposter syndrome works. It takes our very real internal experiences and compares them to our external accomplishments. We see a mismatch between the two and, therefore, decide that our accomplishments were imparted to us by chance instead of being earned. We fear that we are frauds. As if that's not bad enough, we as women have the added layer of living in a culture that perpetually minimizes our achievements, further reinforcing these fears.

As if that's not bad enough, we as women have the added layer of living in a culture that perpetually minimizes our achievements, further reinforcing these fears.

When we succeed in business, people speculate about how many men we slept with to get to the top. We are mistaken for secretaries instead of CEOs, asked to take notes in business meetings despite being the most qualified person in the room. When we attempt to be kind and disarming, we are called *airheads* or *flirts*. Yet, when we are assertive and firm, we are called *bitches*. Our genuine attempts at friendship with men are viewed as *attention seeking* when we don't return their sexual advances. Our valid criticisms of men are dismissed as *irrelevant*, and our criticisms of other women are dismissed as *jealousy* and *spite*. We are blamed for our husbands' infidelity and accused of *using sex as a weapon* when really we are just exhausted from doing it all while receiving no support or compassion.

Is it any surprise that in a world that loves to turn a blind eye to our goodness—or worse, to call it wickedness instead—we feel like

Is it any surprise that, in a world that loves to turn a blind eye to our goodness—or worse, to call it wickedness instead—we feel like imposters?

imposters? It would take self-awareness and resolve of steel to not internalize some of the words that are carelessly tossed our way: *airhead, flirt, attention seeker, jealous, spiteful, loose woman sleeping her way to the top, uptight prude withholding sex to manipulate.* Their voices agree with our own internal voice, the one that is already prone to seeing ourselves as imposters. So, we listen to them and believe. It's no wonder that slowly, painfully, we lose that little girl who believed she could do anything.

The thing is, that little girl was the only one who ever knew the real you. She's the only one who still does. She believed you could do anything because she possessed a deep inner knowing. Before the world convinced you that your goodness depended solely on how others perceived you, she knew your value, your worth. She still does. Self-care is reconnecting with that little girl, that part of you who knows the truth that existed before the lies came in.

For me, it took a lot of therapy to reconnect with her. I've learned that almost every bit of imposter syndrome and insecurity I now carry with me was put there by important people in my life, people who mattered, whose opinions I valued greatly. Those people made me question my goodness and worth. Somewhere along the way, I internalized their opinions. I hear their voices telling me I don't deserve it when I am just about to reach for a big opportunity. I hear them when I am trying to make a new friend, whispering that such people wouldn't like me if they knew what I'm really like. And I hear them as I write these words, wondering out loud why anyone would want to take advice from someone as broken as me.

But with therapy, I am beginning to find a voice that is louder. It is the soft but fierce voice of a little girl who knows who I am and what I'm worth. She clenches her tiny hands into fists and shouts to me: *You are worthy! You are capable! You are kind! You deserve good things, you earned good things, you do good things!* Slowly, I am learning to hear her above those other voices. My weekly tuning in to her voice is a defiant act of self-care. It defies the systems, the people, the policies, the opinions that tell me I am not who that little girl sees in me. Self-care is deciding to see myself through her eyes, the way I did before the world dissolved my trust in her.

But with therapy, I am beginning to find a voice that is louder. It is the soft but fierce voice of a little girl who knows who I am and what I'm worth.

You might not need therapy to find her. Maybe you can do it on your own. Reaching out to her is actually pretty easy. When you're ready, and in your own time, close your eyes and get very still. Imagine an empty room, mostly dark but with a warm, gentle light shining down from above. When you've quieted your mind, ask her, "Will you come here and speak to me?"

It may take her time to step into the light. Depending on how long you've been ignoring or forsaking her, it may not be easy for her to trust you at first. But keep asking. Hold space for her. I'm telling you right now, as someone who has done this in therapy and in the solitude of my own room, it's going to feel incredibly weird. You're going to feel self-conscious, and your internal mechanisms that like to monitor how well you're doing at a

It may take her time to step into the light. Depending on how long you've been ignoring or forsaking her, it may not be easy for her to trust you at first. But keep asking. Hold space for her.

task are going to keep nagging at you, telling you you're not doing it right. Stick with it, anyway. Trust the process.

Eventually, you will get the hang of it. You'll trust yourself, and your inner little girl will trust you, too. That's when you can begin asking her important questions. Questions like:

- What do you need from me?
- Is there any pain you are carrying around?
- If so, what is it? And how do I help you heal?
- How have I let you down?
- What do you like about me?

With time, patience, and stillness of mind, she will begin to answer you. She will show you who she sees in you, and you can begin to heal, to grow, and to evolve together.

Whether you do that work alone or with a therapist, I hope you will start soon. You do not deserve to live your life feeling like a fraud. In a world that will try to make your goodness invisible, you must never fail to see it in yourself.

You are not a fraud.

You are not an imposter.

You have everything you need within you.

Just ask that little girl.

Cultivate Your Truth Trench

- **You are not an imposter or a fraud.** Women are so prone to feeling like imposters when we achieve good things. Self-care is confronting this harmful narrative that undermines self-worth and embracing the truth about our worth, capability, and value instead.
- **Your inner child has never forgotten your worth.** Listen to her. Self-trust and inner confidence arrive when you embrace the inner child who has always believed in you. Engage in introspective practices, such as visualization and meditation, to invite the inner child to surface. Embracing your inner child leads to healing and self-validation.
- **Let your voice be louder than the noise.** Shore up your heart against the noise (both internal and external) that says you aren't good enough. When your voice of self-confidence is louder than the voice of doubt, you are free to believe in yourself, to reach for your goals, and to feel authentic pride when you reach them.
- **Cultivating resilience is an act of self-care.** Prioritize ongoing self-care practices that nurture self-esteem and resilience, and foster a resilient mindset grounded in self-belief and empowerment.

Chapter Thirty-Four

Closed Doors

The door is shut tight, yet here I sit. Knocking again and again, waiting for someone to answer and tell me it's all okay.

One of the biggest obstacles I work through in therapy is my need to chase people who make me feel rejected. Whether that is a friend, a lover, or a stranger on the street, if I don't feel acceptance and approval from them, I will chase them down to get it. This need to be accepted has put me in more unsafe and painful circumstances than I care to think about.

My therapist often asks me to visualize the emotional experiences I'm working through to give them some *metaphoric imagery*. When we work on my need to chase down and receive acceptance, what I see every time is a set of enormous wooden doors standing before me. The doors are at least thirty feet high and made of sturdy, immovable wood. I'm always standing before them, knocking until the crimson blood from my splintered knuckles stains the surface, begging for someone to open up.

I know there will be no answer. But even though I'm aware that my pleading is in vain, I can't tear myself away. I feel rooted to the floor. Stuck. I tell my therapist that I can't walk away because *what if they finally answer the door and I'm not here?* So I sit and wait, staring up at a door that I know will not open.

How many of us are standing in front of doors that we know won't open, willing to trade every ounce of our dignity just to be welcomed in? When did we become women who knock at closed doors as if there aren't rows of doors that would gladly open to us? When did we trade our precious self-worth for a little taste of approval from someone else? We beg for potato chips of worth from strangers, partners, friends, and family instead of filling our plates with worth that comes from within. Then, we wonder why we don't feel full.

My therapist said my tendency to chase, to knock at closed doors, was because I had no sense of self-worth. I remember physically shrinking in my seat at his words. *Impossible*, I thought. *I love myself.* I began rattling off a list of all my accomplishments, pulling them out with a flourish like a magician with his bag of tricks: my PhD, my publications, my business, my children. *What do you mean I have no self-worth? Look at this impressive thing here! And that—how many times have you seen one of those? And look, a rabbit, no wait! It's a pocket watch! Ta-da!*

My therapist sat there, unmoving. Unimpressed.

"Amber," he said, "making a list of things you've accomplished is not evidence of self-worth. It's just a list of things you've done. Tell me what you love about *yourself.* About who you are."

I realized I had nothing except the list I'd already given.

No wonder I chased after praise and approval. No wonder I stood at closed doors, begging for them to open. I was a magician with a bunch of tricks . . .

. . . and no magic.

At least, I believed there was no magic. The long and difficult work of self-care in therapy has been learning how to discover my magic again.

Self-worth is magic—a ward against the harshness of the world. It is the sparkly, supernatural stuff that transcends the bullshit of living. Life is hard. *Living is hard.* The world is full of people and experiences that grind away at our spirit, leaving us unsure of who we are and what we deserve. Self-esteem is the mysterious magic, the elusive power, that allows us to trust and believe in ourselves even when all seems lost, when every door stands closed. In order to stop chasing the wrong people and beating on closed doors, I was going to have to learn how to get my hands on some of that magic.

Self-worth is magic—a ward against the harshness of the world. It is the sparkly, supernatural stuff that transcends the bullshit of living.

That work began with me and my therapist identifying negative beliefs I held about myself and starting to challenge and reframe them. We revisited important memories from my childhood and teenage years, most of them involving the sudden departures of people from my life. Like most of us, I learned early that people can choose to leave your life for any reason at all. They can find a new best friend, a new clique, a new girlfriend. They can even find a new family, choosing to go start a new life with a new spouse and new children who get to see them more than every other weekend. As a child, I thought like a child. When there was no identifiable reason why people left my life, I decided it must be something about me. *I was the reason.*

I carried that with me into adulthood. Whenever abrupt endings came into my life, whether those were breakups, lost jobs, or friends who became enemies, I always believed that the end came because of some deficit in me. *I was the problem.*

I developed a kind of dark magic, I guess. What is the opposite of self-worth? Shame? Self-doubt? Inferiority? Whatever its name, it was cruel and powerful. Through therapy, I had to carefully work backward, reprocessing all those memories through a new lens. It was an uncomfortable and sometimes embarrassing process. It didn't feel great, as a thirty-eight-year-old woman, to sob uncontrollably while sharing stories about being teased by the girls I thought were friends in middle school. Rejected by the boys I liked in high school. I wondered what kind of broken grown-up hasn't gotten over such childish things by now. Why did they still hurt?

My therapist walked me through these memories, these little-t traumas, all the way from childhood to the present. In each story, he asked, "What did *you* do to make that happen? Tell me what *you* did wrong there." Of course, there were plenty of times that I had made mistakes, had contributed to the problem. Those, we processed and set aside. Our focus was on the multitudes of times people treated me indelicately, cruelly even, when I had done nothing wrong. As we broke down story after story of unkindness and closed doors, being unable to identify anything I had done to deserve that treatment, things became clear. The answer was reassuring and horrifying at the same time.

It wasn't about me at all. (Whew!) *Sometimes, people are just cruel.* (Shit.)

It wasn't about me at all. (Whew!) *Sometimes, people are just cruel.* (Shit.)

It's scary to discover that the world is filled with unkind people—people who are unhappy and unhealed, looking to bury their self-hatred into some other willing soul. It was even scarier to realize that, for most of my life, I'd worn a giant "WILLING SOUL" sign on my forehead. But what comforted, what brought sweet relief, was the realization that sometimes people treat others cruelly simply because they can. And it doesn't say anything about my worth, my value, or what I do or do not deserve.

But what comforted, what brought sweet relief, was the realization that sometimes people treat others cruelly simply because they can. And it doesn't say anything about my worth, my value, or what I do or do not deserve.

At my therapist's suggestion, I read *The Four Agreements* by Don Miguel Ruiz. If you haven't read it yet, please add it to your list. It would be such a privilege to think that somehow my words led someone else to read that incredible book. It changed my life. There are, as you might have guessed, four agreements the book says we ought to live by. One of them is to *take nothing personally.* Ruiz suggests that people treat us badly because of their own feelings and beliefs. Nothing anybody does is because of us. It's always about themselves.

It's so easy for us to internalize other people's unkind treatment—to wear their opinions of us like a scarlet letter. But the truth is nothing anyone thinks about us is actually a reflection of who we truly are. Think about it. We, as a society, collectively agree that murder is wrong. Yet, we fundamentally disagree about whether the death penalty—the murder of a murderer—is a morally correct way to execute justice. I actually can't think of a single thing that we as a species have collectively and wholly agreed upon. There is, essentially, no universally agreed-upon truth. Almost everything has nuance, is shaded by people's opinions that were formed by their unique experiences and upbringings. Even the things that *should* be universally agreed upon, like the equality of all people of all genders, sexes, races, and ethnicities, will be contested by people who want to believe "alternative facts." If there is no objective truth, then no one's opinion of you or of me can be universally true, either.

Their opinions *only* say something about them. Never about you.

Crazy, right?

Imposter syndrome and low self-worth have spent a lifetime telling me that everything is my fault, that I deserve to be mistreated. On the other hand, I've heard "self-care gurus" and "life coaches" and "boundary experts" preach that literally nothing is ever my fault, that anyone who disagrees with or disapproves of me is in the wrong. To these gurus, the answer to every problem is going "no contact." To them, the solution is never to work through obstacles with other people, to take accountability or mend fences.

Fulfilling self-care on my journey to claim my self-worth and to stop knocking at closed doors has meant finding the balance between these two competing ideas. I have refined the skill of not taking things personally. I've learned that in every circumstance, other people are interacting with me from their own beliefs about the world. That means that, occasionally, there will be people who will dislike me, reject me, and slam doors in my face simply because they are projecting their worldview onto me and deciding that I fall short. And that still says absolutely nothing about me. Fulfilling self-care means believing that people can disapprove of me and that takes nothing away from my worth or value. I don't have to hate them or feel spurned by their disapproval. I also don't have to be around people who disapprove of me and make me feel small. I don't have to stand at the doors that shut in my face, begging to be let in. I can find doors that open to me willingly instead.

I don't have to hate them or feel spurned by their disapproval. I also don't have to be around people who disapprove of me and make me feel small. I don't have to stand at the doors that shut in my face, begging to be let in. I can find doors that open to me willingly instead.

I've also learned to accept that I

approach people from my beliefs about the world, too. That means that occasionally, I will bring my own friction to the table. Like most of us, I am a broken soul on a journey of healing, of putting myself back together. I will sometimes overreact, misunderstand, or make a big deal out of something very small simply because I'm triggered. Self-care has meant giving myself compassion when that happens—accepting that I cannot, and will not, be perfect. This is the mindset that has brought balance between the competing voices of the imposter syndrome and the toxic self-care internet gurus. I've learned that there *are* some doors that are worth knocking at. Sometimes, doors close for good reason because I caused pain. And, with the gentle knocking of sincerity, openness, and humility, I can try to coax those doors back open.

My journey of self-worth has taught me to use discernment about which doors I knock on these days. I am *worthy and valuable and deserving.* That means I have no business knocking at the doors of people who reject or disapprove of me because of their own beliefs about me and the world. I do not have to beg for potato chips of worth from people who will never truly approve of me anyway.

But! *Because* I am worthy and valuable and deserving, I also deserve to do the work of mending relationships that matter to me. Taking accountability, asking for forgiveness, and knocking on the *right* doors are acts of immeasurable self-care. I deserve to put myself back in right standing with the people who bring me joy, who bring value to my life.

I deserve to put myself back in right standing with the people who bring me joy, who bring value to my life.

Self-worth, working through self-care, guides me to the right doors. It gives me the wisdom to know which doors deserve my knocking and which doors to walk away from, unopened.

That is the real magic.

Cultivate Your Truth Trench

- **Do not stand at closed doors.** It is natural to feel the urge to chase approval from those who make you feel rejected, but from now on, you must fight that urge. Learning not to chase people who slam doors in your face begins with gaining an authentic grasp on your own worth and value.
- **Your worth is inherent; it never leaves you.** Although it is important to feel loved and accepted by others, it's just as important that you cultivate a sense of worth that does not depend on what other people think. Challenge the part of you that wants to believe your worth is measured by external sources. Your worth goes everywhere you go.
- **Other people's opinions say something about them, not about you.** Though it can be difficult, try your best not to take things personally. Other people's behavior and opinions are a reflection of their own beliefs and experiences; they say nothing about your worth.
- **Stand at the *right* doors.** Exercise discernment in relationships, distinguishing between doors worth knocking on for reconciliation and closure and those better left unopened, prioritizing self-respect and emotional well-being in the process.

Chapter Thirty-Five

Neurobland

I am what I call neurodivergent-adjacent.

My husband and my son are delightfully neurodivergent—they both have ADHD—and my son inherited a bit of my anxiety as well. They are eccentric, quirky, and astonishingly talented people who capture my interest in new ways every day. My daughter likely has ADHD, too, but she's still a bit too young to get a diagnosis. Most of my closest friends are on one or more of the spectrums. It seems like neurodivergent people just sort of find their way to me. It's a symbiotic relationship, of sorts. My nearly infallible executive function skills help keep them grounded, and their immeasurable creativity keeps me inspired. It's a perfect fit.

I love the differently abled and differently brained people in my orbit. They add flavor to my life that can sometimes become a little too structured, a little too left-brained. But, in a world that is becoming increasingly filled with the enchantingly neurodivergent, sometimes being neurotypical feels a little . . . dull?

If those people are what the world calls neuro-spicy, I guess that makes me neuro-bland. I am allistic and don't have ADHD. Apart from my anxiety and some mild sensory processing issues, I am yawningly neurotypical. Sometimes, as weird as it sounds, it feels lonely being neurotypical in a house with people who are neurodiverse. The funny little lapses in executive function that are adorable when they happen to my husband and son are annoying when they happen to me. My small lapses in memory, like leaving the house without my keys, or big mistakes like driving us to a cruise port in the wrong state, are just examples of me being careless. That's how I see it, anyway. Nobody else judges me for these stupid mistakes I make. Yet, I beat myself up for them. Sometimes, I wish I had a label I could put on these mistakes. I wish I could blame my occasional inattentiveness, forgetfulness, and obtuseness on some neurodivergent part of my brain. Since I can't, it just feels like I am failing at stuff.

The ubiquity of "therapy speak" and pop psychology online has given us the faulty belief that everything related to mental health must have a label. Labels give us comfort—a way to explain our behavior. Over the years, I have come to realize that I don't need a label for my struggles to be valid. I am an exhausted, perfection-seeking, overachieving Capricorn who lives up to the title. I'm a hot mess a lot of the time, and I make dumb mistakes. Slowly, I'm learning to embrace them. I don't need a label or an explanation for being imperfect. And why am I striving for perfection anyway? It's not an obtainable goal.

I don't need a label or an explanation for being imperfect. And why am I striving for perfection anyway? It's not an obtainable goal.

I've been there when a lot of my loved ones received their diagnoses of ADHD and autism. It seemed like every one of them experienced equal parts of relief and fear. On one hand, they were relieved to finally have an answer, an explanation for the things that just haven't made sense. On the other hand, there was the fear of the unknown, the new normal. The label brought peace; it also brought some anxiety. Over time, I watched all of them leave the fear in the dust. They found true self-understanding for perhaps the first time in their lives. They embraced themselves fully, understanding that what makes them different also makes them dazzlingly unique, gifted, and special. My husband calls his ADHD his superpower. Yes, it can frustrate him at times. But it's his ADHD that gives him many of the incredible gifts that he loves about himself, gifts that I love, too.

It seems a little weird to suggest that neurotypical people might need to go through the same process, but it's a truth I've come to embrace. Just because I am not neurodivergent doesn't mean that I have to apply negative labels to myself instead. I don't have to label myself as *inconsiderate, lazy, absent-minded,* or *self-absorbed* when I make mistakes. I'm just *human*, and human is a neutral term. I make mistakes because I'm human, because I'm exhausted, because my kids finally pushed me over the edge.

It sounds absurd to say that self-care is simply choosing to not assign negative labels to ourselves, but sometimes, I think it may be as simple as that.

I'm just *human*, and human is a neutral term. I make mistakes because I'm human, because I'm exhausted, because my kids finally pushed me over the edge.

Cultivate Your Truth Trench

- **Not everything needs a label.** Challenge the societal pressure to label every aspect of mental health and behavior, understanding that validation and self-acceptance do not require a diagnosis or explanation.
- **You don't have to be perfect to be good.** Shift your focus from striving for perfection to embracing imperfection as a fundamental aspect of being human, and acknowledge that mistakes and shortcomings are inevitable and do not define your worth.
- **Embrace the things that make you special and unique.** Whether you are neurodivergent or neurotypical, you deserve self-understanding and compassion. Strive to embrace your uniqueness and to live wholly as your authentic self.
- **Sensible self-care simplifies things.** Recognize that self-care can be as simple as choosing not to internalize negative labels or expectations, allowing yourself the grace to be human, and acknowledging your inherent worthiness despite perceived flaws or imperfections.

Chapter Thirty-Six

Mom Bods and Muffin Tops

If you already hate this chapter just based on the title, don't worry, I do, too.

It sucks. I know. But we have to talk about it.

Learning to embrace a body that has reached its late thirties, has birthed two children, and has sucked plumpness from the places it belongs and transported it to places it doesn't has been, well, a challenge.

Last year, I started riding a Peloton at my apartment's gym to lose the extra weight I had packed on during my separation from Charlie. (It turns out that drinking wine and baking sugary treats every night doesn't do much for your body *or* your mental health.) I got addicted to the bike pretty quickly, and after a few months of dedication to daily rides, Charlie bought me a Peloton of my own. I rode it every day for three months straight. Sometimes twice a day. I was eating healthy. Drinking less. I endured painful CoolSculpting on my abdominal muscles to try to get back that chiseled look from my youth. After months of hard work and suffering, my body looked pretty good! But I was exhausted, underfed, and in a constant state of soreness that wouldn't go away.

It's hard to stay motivated when you're starving and exhausted. Eventually, I gave up entirely. I stopped riding my bike. Started choosing comfort foods over healthy ones. At first, I felt great! I was finally fed and rested. I felt so good, in fact, that I decided to celebrate by getting back into my wine habit. Slowly, one glass at bedtime turned into two glasses, into three. I began pouring the first glass at dinner instead of bedtime, then while I *made* dinner. That first glass of wine eventually started getting poured the moment I got my kids home from school.

I didn't have a "problem." I wasn't addicted. I was just self-soothing.

It wasn't long before all the weight I lost had piled back on, plus some. I was low on energy and none of my pants fit anymore. I was ashamed and defeated. My fresh new start and all my hard work had been for nothing, and soon, I was completely depressed.

About two months ago, I decided it was time to do something about my body, once and for all. But this time, I was going to tackle my *mind* first. I wasn't going back into an unrealistic diet and fitness routine that was going to take more away from me than it gave. Furthermore, I was going to get my head right about a few things. It was time to finally address the unhealthy relationship I had, and have always had, with my body.

It was time to finally address the unhealthy relationship I had, and have always had, with my body.

Toxic gym culture, dishonest social media influencers, and, surprisingly, even the body positivity movement have made women's relationships with their bodies so much harder than they have to be. Gym culture tells us to work out more and eat less carbs and we'll get the bodies we desire. Body positivity culture tells us to love our bodies, just like that! Magically erase years of shame and disgust toward our bodies by just *deciding* to like them one day. Social media influencers tell us to just buy this super-green protein powder, or try this incredible appetite suppressant, and with no work at all our fitness dreams can be realized.

It doesn't help that millennial women like me didn't grow up with Lizzo and Tess Holiday to show us that bodies come in all shapes and sizes and all can be beautiful. Glamorous, even! We grew up in a time when the lead in every movie was rail thin and perfectly sculpted. Actresses with any other body type were cast as the quirky and bookish sidekick or the fat-and-funny comic relief but never the love interest. Was there any hope for us to *not* develop disordered thinking about our bodies when that was all we saw?

Was there any hope for us to *not* develop disordered thinking about our bodies when that was all we saw?

My new fitness journey, the one based on realistic expectations and a healthy attitude toward my body, had to begin with my mind. My body is fundamentally different now than it was when I was in my twenties. I have stretch marks. There is the diastases recti that still hasn't fully healed. My metabolism is slower. I used to be able to just skip a meal if I was feeling fluffy and I'd drop three to four pounds instantly. These days, paradoxically, I have to eat *more* in order to lose weight because now my body just stops metabolizing when I don't eat. It would be absurd for me to expect my body to respond to diet and exercise the way it used to, especially now that I've had children.

Self-care, when it comes to my physical fitness, has been a journey of acceptance.

I've accepted that my body *could* look exactly the way I want it to look, but at this point in my life, it just takes too much sacrifice to maintain. My body does not naturally want to be 120 pounds anymore. Struggling to reach that weight again will only lead to failure and misery.

Acceptance has meant recalibrating. I've had to learn to reach for what is possible within reason, within limits. *What can I do to reach a place where I am happy with my body and can still enjoy my life?*

Acceptance has meant recalibrating. I've had to learn to reach for what is possible within reason, within limits. *What can I do to reach a place where I am happy with my body and can still enjoy my life?*

It's a mindset thing. I call it my sustainable fitness plan. It's an approach that prioritizes my long-term health and wellness over short-term results or aesthetics. It means choosing workouts that feel good and that energize me rather than punishing myself with intense exercise that I dread. It means feeding my body nourishing foods that sustain me rather than restricting or limiting myself. And it means being kind and compassionate to my body rather than constantly beating myself up for not looking a certain way. Finally, it also means forgiving myself for not being able to accept my body exactly as it is with complete unconditional love. I'll get there one day, I hope. But that's a journey that will require patience and a lot of grace.

Finally, it also means forgiving myself for not being able to accept my body exactly as it is, with complete unconditional love. I'll get there one day, I hope. But that's a journey that will require patience and a lot of grace.

Self-care, as it relates to my body, has meant accepting that two things can be true at once. I can have an ideal body image that I want to achieve while still practicing self-compassion and having realistic expectations. I *do* have a certain way I want to look, and I get bummed out when I don't look that way. Contrary to what I think the body positivity movement wants us to believe, some of us will always struggle with our body image. I can't just pretend to be happy with every dimple and unwanted roll. Trying to force myself into that mindset of complete body acceptance just leaves me feeling defeated. At risk of completely exhausting the metaphor, this kind of empty-calorie self-care mantra is unable to nourish our bodies or our souls. It leaves us with the sensation of fullness but cannot actually make us fulfilled. Like potato chips, it might feel good in the moment, but it leaves us hungry for more.

So, I have to accept that it's okay to be dissatisfied with how my body looks but also understand that fitness is a journey that will take time. Rather than abusing my body with restricted calories and overexertion to get quick results, I have to play the long game. I have to get my mind right. In the meantime, as I slowly sculpt my body into a form I am happy with, I'll work on accepting my body in the *now*, exactly as it is. After all, I can't hate my body into making it look the way I want it to look.

After all, I can't hate my body into making it look the way I want it to look.

This gentle work of self-care has slowly but surely begun the process of healing my relationship with my body. I've left a lot of my negative body-talk behind me. I've also let go of trying to achieve the Zen-like, unconditional acceptance of my body as it is right now. I've embraced the concept of *body neutrality*, instead. I tell myself things like:

> I won't love my body every day, but I can appreciate what it does for me.

I don't judge myself on days I don't like my body. It's normal, and it'll pass.

I try my best to nourish my body in a healthy way, but I am also allowed to enjoy my favorite foods.

I can't hate myself into health or fitness, but through loving myself and giving myself grace, I'll get there.

This process of embracing body neutrality has finally gotten me to a place of real, sustainable health and fitness. I'm following a nutrition plan (which I definitely will never refer to as a diet) that helps me choose foods I love that still nourish and fuel my body. I have a fitness plan that gives me days off to recover and that includes exercise I actually enjoy doing, even if those exercises aren't as efficient or calorie burning as others. I am becoming consistent because I actually look forward to working out and because my body is fed and rested.

I am worthy of love, kindness, dignity, and respect at any weight, and I deserve those things even if I'm not happy with my body in its present form.

I am learning that some days, my pants are going to fit tightly. Some days, I'm going to hate everything I try on. *It's okay. That's normal. Breathe. You'll get there eventually.* I'm learning to finally accept that my body does not determine my value. I am worthy of love, kindness, dignity, and respect at any weight, and I deserve those things even if I'm not happy with my body in its present form.

Incredibly, it's been through acceptance and letting go that I've finally begun to see real, lasting results. Of all my self-care journeys, this one has been undoubtedly the hardest. The world has done such an unconscionable disservice to our relationship with our bodies.

That indoctrination began when we were very small, and it's in our faces every day. The only self-care that is worth anything when it comes to our bodies is the kind that is born out of self-compassion.

You cannot hate your body into health and fitness, my darling friend.

That work must be done through love.

The only self-care that is worth anything when it comes to our bodies is the kind that is born out of self-compassion.

Cultivate Your Truth Trench

- **Bodies change.** That's normal, and it's okay. It can be difficult to let go of rigid beliefs about your body, but it's time to begin the work of doing so. Give yourself grace if you struggle to embrace your body as it changes over time, especially after childbirth or as you age, but remember to also give yourself permission to embrace the changes as a symbol of a life well lived.
- **Practice gentle, sustainable fitness over punishing your body.** Embrace the reality of your body's natural changes and limitations, letting go of the pursuit of unattainable ideals and instead focusing on sustainable fitness practices that prioritize long-term health and wellness.
- **Body neutrality is a healthy way to heal your relationship with your body.** Adopt a mindset of body neutrality, acknowledging that it's okay to have days when you don't love your body while still appreciating its functionality and worth beyond appearance.
- **Only self-love can do the job.** Embrace acceptance of your body at any stage, understanding that self-worth and value are not determined by physical appearance and that real, lasting results in health and fitness come from a foundation of self-love and acceptance.

SECTION VI

Over Coffee:

Self-Care in Our Communication

Chapter Thirty-Seven

Axelrod's Tournament

I have to talk to you about computer science for a second. Stick with me, it'll make sense.

In 1980, a man named David Axelrod held a computer coding tournament. The world's top computer scientists were asked to develop algorithms that could win a computer simulation of something called the Prisoner's Dilemma.

(I misspoke. I have to talk to you about psychology first, then computer science.)

The Prisoner's Dilemma was this really interesting psychology experiment done in the 1970s. In the experiment, two volunteer participants were told that they had been arrested for committing the same crime and would be interviewed separately. The rules of the experiment were fairly simple: without knowing what the other participant would do, both participants had to decide whether to confess to the crime or stay silent. If they both stayed silent, they both got a small punishment. If they both confessed, they both got a medium punishment. But, if one confessed and the other stayed silent, the one who confessed got no punishment, and the one who stayed silent got a big punishment. The dilemma was that both participants had to decide (without knowing what the other participant would do) whether to look out for themselves or to cooperate with the other participant in hopes of both getting the best outcome.

Axelrod's tournament replicated the Prisoner's Dilemma experiment but with computer algorithms instead of human participants. The goal was to see which algorithm could "win" the tournament by outsmarting all the other algorithms in the Prisoner's Dilemma. Although the competitors submitted algorithms that contained thousands of lines of code, the winning algorithm was called *Tit-for-tat* and contained only two simple lines. To paraphrase, they looked this:

Step 1: Always cooperate first.

Step 2: Then, do whatever your opponent did in the previous round.

So, the Tit-for-tat algorithm always started by cooperating. If the opponent algorithm chose to also cooperate, they would go back and forth in a mutually beneficial paradigm of cooperation. However, if the other algorithm decided to "play dirty" by acting in its own self-interest instead of cooperating, the Tit-for-tat algorithm would then stop cooperating as well. This would continue until the opponent decided to resume cooperating, and at that time, the Tit-for-tat algorithm would cooperate, too. If we put this into modern-day *human* vernacular, it would be something like this: "I will always seek to cooperate with other people, and as long as others respond in kind, I will continue to cooperate. But if someone chooses to be self-serving, unkind, or malicious, I will match that energy."

This unexpectedly simple algorithm taught scientists a lot about cooperation, competition, and communication. We so often find ourselves in situations where we have to weigh our own interests against the interests of others. Sometimes, with very little time to deliberate, we must decide if we are going to act in a way that best serves our own needs or if we are going to work with other people and compromise, working toward what serves the needs of everyone. How we go about making those decisions can have a substantial impact on how we view ourselves and our relationships with others.

To bring the point home with something related (and probably a bit more familiar), let's return to the movie *A Beautiful Mind.* John Nash (played by Russell Crowe) and his male comrades went to a bar and spotted a beautiful blonde with several "less attractive" friends. All the boys wanted to ask the blonde to dance, but Nash pushed back. He told them that if they all went for the blonde, she would reject all but one of them. Then, when the rejected boys went for the other friends, the friends would reject them, too, because no one likes being second pick. His advice, instead, was that none of the boys go for the blonde. They should all go for the other girls so that they weren't competing with one another. "We won't get in each other's way, and we won't insult the other girls. It's the only way to win, it's the only way we all get laid," he says.

In this example, Nash communicates the same concept as the algorithms in Alexrod's tournament. However crass the example may be, it shows us that sometimes, thinking of what's best for the group can help us achieve what is best for ourselves, too.

How we choose to operate and communicate in our relationships with others is a really huge deal. It's something that's been on my mind through my entire healing and self-care journey. We have to walk this fine line between looking out for own interests while existing in a world that is composed of many other people who have competing interests.

The takeaway message from the two previous examples is that perhaps self-care looks like establishing our "rules of engagement" for how we engage with other people. For me, that has largely meant figuring out how to communicate with people in order to meet my own needs while also caring for theirs.

Step One in my rules of engagement is the same as the Tit-for-tat algorithm in Axelrod's tournament. Like the algorithm, I always begin conversations with the intent to cooperate and do no harm. I try to be kind and fair and to communicate in good faith. I fail at this sometimes, and I have to try again. But as far as intent goes, my first rule is to never enter a conversation seeking to harm the other person. I used to stop at Step One. I told myself I was being a good communicator and taking the "higher road" when I decided to continue being kind even when someone didn't return the favor. I became a doormat, letting people walk all over me in the name of "kindness."

But as far as intent goes, my first rule is to never enter a conversation seeking to harm the other person.

Now I've added Step Two, which is also in-line with the Tit-for-tat algorithm. If the other person continues to be kind and show respect, we will go back and forth in a mutual good-faith dialogue. But if the other person chooses to be cruel, nasty, or disrespectful, I will "do whatever the opponent did in the previous round." Meaning, I will not be afraid to serve up some attitude, too. I will match their energy unapologetically.

I will match their energy unapologetically.

I have my limits. There is only so far I am willing to foray into the pit with them. They *will* understand, though, that I will not smile through their insults. I will be unafraid to revoke my kindness.

I am doing self-care when I begin my conversations by communicating with kindness. I'm a highly sensitive person who doesn't like conflict, so setting the tone early by modeling kindness helps me avoid unnecessary squabbles with others. When I get super dysregulated and approach a conversation from a place that isn't kind or constructive, I do harm to myself twice. The first harm happens when I create a tense atmosphere that makes me anxious and upset (and that could have been avoided). The second harm happens when I harm someone I care about and put a blemish on our relationship. Anything I do that causes me stress or alienates me from others is not loving or caring toward myself. So, self-care must include kindness. But! I am also doing self-care when I refuse to be a doormat. I do not deserve to be treated unkindly or disrespectfully. I deserve gentleness, patience, and cooperation. Self-care, then, must also include a little bit of "fuck around and find out."

I am also doing self-care when I refuse to be a doormat. I do not deserve to be treated unkindly or disrespectfully. I deserve gentleness, patience, and cooperation. Self-care, then, must also include a little bit of "fuck around and find out."

Step Three in my rules of engagement, which has proven the hardest of all for me personally, harkens back to Nash and the blonde. When it comes to communication, I have to understand that I am speaking to another human being who has their own needs and interests. If I care about that person, I have to communicate with them in a way that solves our problems cooperatively. There is a lot of toxic self-care nonsense out there that tells us that only *our* needs matter. They perpetuate the idea that we should put ourselves first no matter what, validate our own behavior no matter what (even when we are dysregulated and harmful), and if other people don't like it, to hell with them. It promotes an attitude toward others that is selfish, rigid, inflexible, and unwilling to compromise. (I'm sure you've met at least one person who has adopted this kind of attitude, and I'd bet you don't like it.)

I'm here to tell you that treating people in a way that disregards their feelings is not self-care or self-love. True self-care prioritizes relationships, recognizing that getting along with the people we love is a way we also show love to ourselves. So, we have to communicate in a way that fosters respect, empathy, and the other person's interests while also considering our own.

I'm learning that to care for myself and for others means listening with intent and empathy, framing issues as a shared problem to be solved, and being open to compromise. I have to strive to understand other people's experiences and emotions, acknowledge their perspectives, and try to find common ground that benefits us both. At the same time, I must also make sure that I am weighing out my needs with theirs and watching to see if they are doing the same. I don't have to give unconditional cooperation and kindness to someone who won't do the same for me. It's not about winning. It's not about who's right or wrong. It's about doing what's best for myself *and* for the people I care about.

Self-care is being a bridge, not a doormat.

Cultivate Your Truth Trench

- **Having "rules of engagement" helps you navigate difficult conversations.** Similar to the Tit-for-tat algorithm, establishing rules of engagement in communication can guide our interactions with others, especially when conversations get difficult. Starting with kindness and cooperation sets a positive tone, but being willing to match the energy of others when faced with disrespect or unkindness (within reason) can be equally important for our mental health and well-being.
- **There is a time for cooperation and a time for assertiveness.** Self-care involves balancing cooperation with assertiveness. While being kind and empathetic is important, it's equally vital to assert boundaries and stand up for yourself when necessary. Advocate for yourself while still treating others with respect.
- **Maintaining connection with those we love is an act of self-care.** True self-care prioritizes relationships by recognizing that maintaining healthy connections with others contributes to our well-being. Communication should foster respect, empathy, and consideration for both parties' needs, aiming for mutual understanding and compromise.
- **Be a bridge, not a doormat.** Self-care is about being a bridge between your own needs and the needs of others rather than being a doormat. It's about finding a balance between advocating for yourself and fostering harmonious relationships *with the right people,* ultimately promoting mutual growth and well-being.

Chapter Thirty-Eight
Heard

"You seem like someone who knows how to use your voice. You just don't know how to be heard."

When my therapist said these words to me, it was like a bomb went off. I was telling him how I often feel like people don't notice or respond to my needs. That time in particular, I was talking about my husband, Charlie. This was many years ago, prior to our separation and at a time when I felt completely hopeless about our future. I told my therapist that it seemed like I'd told Charlie over and over what I needed from him in order to be happy in our marriage, but no matter what I said, nothing seemed to change. I thought maybe I was a bad communicator, but according to my therapist, it was bigger than that. It wasn't that I didn't know how to communicate. I communicated all the time! The problem was that I didn't know how to communicate in a way that enabled people to hear me.

How many of us feel like we are constantly talking—sharing about ourselves, being vulnerable, opening up to others, and yearning to feel less alone—but we're never quite feeling heard? Navigating this deep loneliness can be so hard. Learning how to communicate in ways that allow us to be heard is even harder.

I have lots of unhealthy ways of communicating. I can lash out when I feel stung by someone's words, however small or unintentional they might have been. If someone's words hit me like a powderpuff, I'll drop an anvil on their heads. On the other hand, sometimes, instead of lashing out, I completely clam up, and not in the healthy *I'm just going to take some time and process my thoughts* kind of way. It's the *I really want to talk about this right now, but I'm going to stonewall you instead* way that, if I'm being honest, is more about punishing the other person than anything else. Sometimes, I get flustered and lose the plot. Instead of focusing on the conversation at hand, I start tossing grenades from the past into the equation. Other times, I will be totally focused on the present topic but will domineer the conversation and not let the other person say their piece.

None of these things help me be heard.

I'm learning that *speaking* isn't the same as *communicating*. I can talk until my jaws are sore, but unless I am saying out loud what I actually need from the people around me, and saying it in a way that enables them to hear me, I am not really communicating.

This has been a difficult, humbling lesson.

Communication has been a big theme of this book. It shows up in almost every arena of our lives, from our romantic relationships to our families, to our friends and careers. We deserve to be heard. For some of us, self-care is the difficult work of learning healthier ways of communicating so that we *can* be heard.

We deserve to be heard. For some of us, self-care is the difficult work of learning healthier ways of communicating so that we *can* be heard.

Some of the steps toward healthier communication have already been discussed. We've talked about speaking our needs out loud—saying exactly what we need in clear terms instead of expecting people to be mind readers. We've talked about having the right people at our table, people who know how to listen with interest and respond with empathy. We've also talked about having the courage to stand up for ourselves even when it might come with some backlash, even when it's scary.

Those things sound very empowering. They are the things that require a lot of courage and a little hubris. Perhaps what we've failed to talk about until this point is the stuff that requires humility. The stuff that makes us take an unflinching look at the ways we communicate poorly or anemically and choose to change. There are several barriers to communication that make it hard for people to hear us. If we engage in any of these, the difficult, humbling work of self-care is learning new ways to communicate.

We have to learn to stop being passive aggressive (and by *we* I most definitely mean *I*). Passive aggressive remarks happen when we take what we mean and strip it of its vulnerability. So, when I say to a friend, "I know my feelings don't matter to you at all, so I don't even know why I'm bringing this up," I'm taking away my own vulnerability (*my friend doesn't care about my feelings*) and turning that vulnerability into an attack. When I start the conversation with an attack, all I'm doing is causing resentment and breaking down the conversation even further. People can't hear us when we start the conversation that way. We have to learn how to express ourselves without being passive aggressive. And, somewhat unfortunately, that means being vulnerable. Vulnerability means saying what we mean—being unafraid to be honest and raw. I need to tell my friend,

"I feel reluctant to share my feelings with you because I feel like you don't really listen or care. That hurts me and makes me shut down. But I really need to share how I'm feeling so that we can resolve it. Can you be present with me and take what I say to heart?"

Sharing with vulnerability instead of passive aggressiveness helps us avoid the next barrier to communication, which is the *suppress and explode* cycle. The suppress and explode cycle is exactly what it sounds like. We shove our feelings down, biting our tongues and refusing to speak about them until, one day, something happens that makes us explode outward, destroying anything in our path.

Pushing our feelings down and hiding them from the world is a trauma response. Someone from our past made us believe that our feelings were stupid, invalid, or a burden, so we stopped sharing. Now, we hold everything in until it comes erupting out like a cannon ball. When this happens to me, I end up exploding over something incredibly small. This leads to a lot of confusion and misunderstandings in my relationships. Also, to be honest, it makes me feel like an idiot. I don't want to be standing there in my kitchen screaming at my husband about not cleaning up the dishes like he said he would. That makes me feel ridiculous and small because screaming over one small oversight *is* ridiculous and small. But the problem was never the dishes still piled in the sink. The problem was that he said he would take care of something and then let me down again. The problem was resentment that had built up after stuffing it down a hundred times before.

If I would address these small offenses, like the dishes, when they happen, my husband could actually help me with them. I could bring these things up constructively while I'm calm, not after I've already flipped my lid and cursed him out a dozen times in my own head.

He can't hear me when I'm losing my mind over what he believes is just one mistake. Sharing my concerns in real time, when I'm calm and composed, helps him be able to hear me and to respond with empathy instead of defensiveness.

Another barrier to communication is *blame shifting*, which is a super uncomfy one to work on. It's *so hard* to sit in the discomfort of our own actions, especially in very complex, emotionally dense relationships. There is seldom only one person at fault, so when a spouse, a friend, a family member, or a coworker brings something to our attention that we need to take accountability for, our first impulse is usually to blame shift. We remember all the ways they failed us, insulted us, or let us down and how we stayed silent about it. When they have the *absolute audacity* to point out our failings, we want to throw all their shortcomings in their face.

I have something really unpleasant to tell you about that. You're going to hate it: *It's not their fault that we didn't tell them when they let us down, and they aren't obligated to not share our shortcomings with us just because we didn't share theirs with them.*

If we choose to keep our discontent with other people to ourselves in the name of keeping the peace, we can't suddenly be ready to air out our grievances when they point out the ways we've let them down. Suddenly pointing out the harms another person has done to us when they, in good faith, bring our harms to our attention is shifting the blame to get the attention off ourselves. We can't expect people to hear us if we only bring up their shortcomings when we're in the hot seat. We have to learn to receive critical feedback with grace—without blame shifting—in order to be heard.

We also have to avoid being *overly critical*, invaliding or dismissing other people's needs, making sweeping assumptions, and playing mind tricks like gaslighting or guilt-tripping. Honestly, do you respond well when people use these tactics on you? Of course not. But as we all know, when we are hurt or angry, it's easy to justify using those tactics ourselves.

The uncomfortable truth is that using these barriers to communication is not only bad for our relationships. It's also bad for our self-esteem, self-confidence, and self-respect. Communicating this way shoves metaphorical cotton balls in people's ears. They simply cannot hear us when we engage this way. To be honest, they probably will begin to not like us that much. How are we to build a healthy self-esteem when we sense the people we care about pulling away from us, choosing to create distance rather than deal with our unhealthy ways of communicating?

The uncomfortable truth is that using these barriers to communication is not only bad for our relationships. It's also bad for our self-esteem, self-confidence, and self-respect.

You deserve to be heard. I deserve it, too. We deserve to have relationships with others that build our self-esteem, not that risk tearing it down. We can't control how other people will respond to us, and there will always be people who choose not to hear us even when our communication is immaculate. But we can control ourselves. Self-care is communicating in ways that open people's ears rather than close them.

There are plenty of people who want to hear you.

Sincerity, vulnerability, openness, and humility are the tools that make it possible.

Cultivate Your Truth Trench

- **Strive for communicating, not just talking.** Merely talking isn't the same as effective communication. It's crucial to express your needs openly and clearly in a way that enables others to truly hear you. Communication involves vulnerability, sincerity, and the ability to convey your needs in healthy ways.
- **Self-care is using self-restraint in how you communicate with others.** Identify and overcome barriers to communication such as being overly critical, making assumptions, or engaging in manipulative tactics like gaslighting. These behaviors not only damage relationships but also erode self-esteem and self-respect. Although it can be difficult to unlearn deeply entrenched habits, it is good to begin working to reject these barriers to communication and find healthier ways to communicate instead.
- **Communication is a two-way street.** Self-care involves communicating in ways that foster understanding, empathy, and mutual respect. Cultivate sincerity, vulnerability, and humility to create meaningful connections. You deserve relationships with people who are willing to engage in these types of conversations, even when it is difficult.
- **You deserve to be heard.** While you can't control other people's responses, you can control how you communicate. Prioritize sincerity and openness to create spaces where your voice can be heard and respected. Then, if they still don't hear you, that's on them.

Chapter Thirty-Nine

Apology in Word and in Deed

One of the things I remember most from my childhood is the quickness and sincerity of apologies in my family.

There was no ego. No stubbornness. Apologies were given freely. There was no fear of things being left unresolved because no matter how bad they got, there would be an apology—a true and heartfelt reckoning for harms that were done. Apologies didn't always come immediately, but they always came.

As I got older, I began hearing people say that actions speak louder than words. I learned that "sorry" is a verb—you say you're sorry by the way you change your behavior. It's how you show people that you really regret what you said or did. You commit to never causing that harm again, and then you hold true to your word. I noticed that people in the "actions speak louder than words" camp seemed to be jaded by spoken apologies, feeling that such things have little value and that changed behaviors are far more important than words.

But don't words matter, too?

We live in a world where people don't like admitting they're wrong. Apologies, I learned through the years, are much harder to come by than they were in my childhood home. It seemed like people would do just about anything to avoid saying the words, "I'm sorry." And I didn't really understand it. What could be so hard about saying two very small words?

It seems what people have less of a problem doing is "showing you" their apology. They buy flowers, or text you a funny meme. Romantic partners set up an elaborate date with all your favorite foods and activities. Friends invite you to brunch for some "girl time." Bosses throw a casual Friday pizza party.

A few years ago, a family member who was living with Charlie and me did something that was really hurtful to both of us. For that person's protection, I don't want to get into the details of it. But it was a bad enough situation that it led me to finally reach out to a therapist and get some help (so, at least I'm grateful for that).

The next day, when the dust had settled, he came downstairs while I was making dinner and did a few things to keep my kids (then babies) busy so I could cook. It was so kind and helpful and something I really appreciated because I was overwhelmed between the babies and the brisket. I felt the frosty resentment I'd been holding on to over the last twenty-four hours start to melt away. Later that night, I remember saying to Charlie, "I think that coming downstairs to help me with the kids was his way of apologizing. He's too proud to actually say sorry, so that was how he said it instead." It wasn't as satisfying as a heartfelt apology, but it was something. And for that, I felt a little better.

Still, I went to sleep feeling disturbed. The warm feelings from earlier began to cool, and something just wasn't sitting right with me. I was discomforted not only by my family member's lack of a real apology but by my own reaction to it. Yes, doing something helpful as a way to say you're sorry (without actually saying it) is good. But didn't we miss a step? Aren't the good deeds supposed to come *after* the apology? Like, the sincere *spoken* apology? When did I become comfortable with accepting an apologetic action without an actual apology? And when did I start making excuses for people who didn't care enough to look me in the eyes and acknowledge the harm they'd done? As I looked back, I realized I had been doing that a lot. I gave apologies freely but accepted so much less in return.

I let people off the hook without apologizing to me because "actions speak louder than words." I would point out how they were being so kind to me now, offering to help me, being more sensitive. That's an apology, right? And, well, yes, it is. I'm not here to belittle the actions that people take to show that they are sorry and willing to change. That said, I need words, I need accountability, and frankly, I deserve it. When people give actions in lieu of an apology, that's potato chips. That's high-trans-fat, grease-coated flotsam that feels good in the moment but that doesn't satisfy. Self-care is insisting on the fulfilling nourishment of a real, spoken apology. It is expecting that kind of apology from others, receiving it gracefully when it is given, and freely giving that kind of apology when it is our turn.

Self-care is insisting on the fulfilling nourishment of a real, spoken apology. It is expecting that kind of apology from others, receiving it gracefully when it is given, and freely giving that kind of apology when it is our turn.

A nourishing apology has several important characteristics. First of all, it is specific. The person giving the apology clearly states the things they said or did that caused harm. It's never "I'm sorry you felt like I was dismissive." It is "I'm sorry I was dismissive to you; you didn't deserve to be treated that way."

Second, nourishing apologies provide an explanation. The person giving the apology doesn't give excuses, but rather, they help give context to diffuse any misunderstandings. After the explanation, they give the person who was harmed the opportunity to elaborate on how the harm made them feel, and then extend apologies for anything new that comes up through that conversation. They prioritize and empathize with the feelings of the person receiving the apology.

Third, the person giving the apology offers amends or steps to repair the harm they caused. This is where they make a change in the present *and* sincerely commit to continued change in the future.

Lastly, nourishing apologies are delivered with sincerity and authenticity. They cannot be self-serving or used only to get the person apologizing out of hot water. The person offering the apology needs to demonstrate that they have reflected on the harm they've caused, have come to feel remorse or regret, and are ready to take real accountability.

If we are not giving and receiving these kinds of specific, empathetic, authentic apologies when they are legitimately owed, we are not engaging in true self-care.

If we are not giving and receiving these kinds of specific, empathetic, authentic apologies when they are legitimately owed, we are not engaging in true self-care. Loving ourselves and caring for our well-being means being in right standing with people. Unresolved harm can significantly damage our relationships with other people. It's important that we learn to give and receive real, spoken apologies—the nourishing kind that are a salve to wounded relationships.

Actions speak louder than words, but only after the words are spoken.

Cultivate Your Truth Trench

- **Verbal apologies are important for reconciliation.** Make verbal apologies a priority in your communication with others and expect the same in return. Acknowledging harm and expressing remorse through spoken words are important parts of maintaining healthy relationships.
- **Actions and words go hand in hand; one is not more important than the other.** While actions can complement apologies, ensure that verbal apologies accompany kind gestures. Recognize that both actions and words play crucial roles in effective communication and reconciliation.
- **Apologies should prioritize the feelings of the person who was harmed.** When you apologize to others, make sure you focus on their feelings and not yours. And when receiving apologies, insist that they demonstrate empathy and understanding of how they made you feel. The apologizing person should always listen actively, empathize with the harmed person's experience, and demonstrate genuine concern for their well-being.
- **Apologies don't have to be scary.** Make genuine apologies a priority in your communication with others. Unresolved harm can strain relationships and compromise your well-being. While you may think that avoiding the hard conversations will protect your feelings, letting conflict fester only harms you and your relationships in the end.
- **Remember, you may not need to resolve every conflict.** Sometimes, you have to draw boundaries and walk away. So, please remember that this advice is only for relationships where you genuinely want to stay in communion with the other person.

Chapter Forty

Self

I remember how confused Charlie looked the first time I told him, "I'm not in *self* right now. I'd like to postpone this conversation until I feel more self-like." We were just beginning to discuss the possibility of ending our separation and reconciling our marriage. He wasn't quite used to my therapy lingo yet.

My therapist and I do a lot of Parts Work therapy. Parts Work therapy says that we have a "core self," plus a host of various internal parts that make up our personality and worldview. The goal of Parts Work therapy is to bring all these parts together in harmony for healing, personal growth, and fruitful relationships with others.

It turns out that we all have a basic understanding of Parts Work, even if we've never heard the term before. We say things like "Part of me wants to give it another shot, but part of me wants to just move on already." When we use this kind of language, we demonstrate that we recognize different parts of ourselves—parts that have very different priorities and interests. In Parts Work therapy, we work toward recognizing all the different parts that make up our core *self*. We name them, ask them what their goals and priorities are, and work toward understanding what purpose they serve for our overall well-being.

I've learned to identify several of my parts. I have one that we call The Manager. Her role is to look out for me and keep my other parts in check. I have another one we call The Compassionate Femme. She holds my traditional values that I have mostly discarded but that are still a part of who I am. There is also the part we call The Joker. She loves to create what looks like mayhem, but those actions are actually just her attempt to solve my problems through whatever means necessary.

In Parts Work, all parts are good parts. There are *no bad parts.*

In Parts Work, all parts are good parts. There are *no bad parts.* However, every part has certain goals that only it cares about. Although none of my parts are bad, it might not be the best idea to let certain parts handle situations that don't suit their needs and goals. For example, I mentioned that my Joker part will use whatever means necessary to solve my problems. If I get pulled over by a police officer for speeding, a "reasonable solution" according to The Joker would be for me to speed off and evade the ticket. To a part who cares more about the present problem than future consequences, speeding away is a really useful option. It for sure solves the immediate problem. And if the scenario was different and my life were in danger, this part's impulse to run away would be correct. But, obviously, speeding away from a police officer after I've broken the law does not solve my problem in the long run. My Joker part's interest in getting me to speed away doesn't make that part *bad.* It just means that part isn't the one I want handling a situation like that.

An important component of Parts Work therapy is learning to identify when we have a part that is activated and figuring out if that part is speaking or acting in a way that serves our best interest. If not, we need to try our best to get back to a place of *self* before that part does any real damage.

The self is the unified whole where the goals and needs of all the parts come together and create balance. When I am in self, there are no other parts screaming for my attention, trying to get me to meet their very unique and (possibly) contextually inappropriate needs. We need to be in a state of self when the stakes are high because that is when we are the most balanced, the best able to determine what is the healthiest choice of word or action.

How do we know when we are in a state of self? There are actually eight traits, eight C's, that come along with being in self. They are **calmness, curiosity, clarity, compassion, confidence, courage, creativity**, and **connectedness**. Yes, I know, it's a lot. But once you've learned to recognize them and to know when you are in self and when you're not, you'll watch your communication and relationships begin to flourish.

I'm learning to recognize that when I am the opposite of the eight C's—when I'm dysregulated, closed off, unclear, uncaring, unconfident, fearful, uninspired, and avoidant—it's not a good time to have important conversations. These are the times when I start engaging in all those barriers to communication we discussed earlier. My conversations devolve, relationships get strained, damage is done. All my parts, even the ones who display these negative traits, are *good parts,* but many of them also happen to be trauma bearers, fear holders. They respond to people and circumstances from a place of self-protection. Their sole purpose is to keep me safe and whole, and they do not care whom they have to offend or alienate in order to do that.

The self understands relationships. It understands that it is important that we get along with others, resolve issues, and mend fences.

When we communicate with other people, particularly if the conversation is heated, we can ask ourselves if we feel the presence of these eight C's of self. If we are in self, we have the green light to move forward with the conversation. If we are not, it may be a good idea to wait to have the conversation until we are more in sync with our inner selves. Applying this simple rule has helped me cultivate healthier relationships with both myself and others. When I approach a conversation from a place of self, I'm more likely to be received positively because the qualities of our true selves are inherently admirable. The person I'm talking to usually reflects these qualities back to me, showing me the warmth, openness, and empathy that I'm showing them.

When this happens, it lifts my self-esteem and makes me feel truly valued. My sense of self-worth soars as I see my relationships grow deeper and more meaningful thanks to healthy, constructive communication.

But perhaps what can have the deepest, most meaningful impact on my self-worth is how I communicate with *myself.* Of course, how I talk to other people is important, but what about how I talk to myself? Am I being kind? Honest? Compassionate? Am I approaching myself *in a state of self*—one in which I embody calmness, curiosity, clarity, compassion, confidence, courage, creativity, and connectedness? Or, is my inner dialogue filled with self-loathing, insecurity, and angst?

Of course, how I talk to other people is important, but what about how I talk to myself? Am I being kind? Honest? Compassionate?

If there is anything you and I deserve, dear reader, it is to speak to ourselves with the same gentle tenderness that we give to the people we love most. Frankly, I think the only way we can hope to show up in our relationships as our true, authentic, and utterly fulfilled selves is if we are bathing ourselves in that tenderness every day.

Why? Because our parts each carry their own stories. Some carry trauma. Some harbor bad memories we stuffed so far down that we've forgotten, but they remember. Some parts have even come to distrust us after years of feeling ignored or invalidated. And before you say, *But, Amber, no one can invalidate their own feelings even if those feelings come from a part,* have you ever felt a strong emotion about something—maybe hurt, or embarrassment, or anger—and said to yourself, "I'm being stupid for being this upset over something like that"?

Don't you lie to me. We both know you have.

That is how easily we gaslight our parts. How easily we invalidate them. How easily we erode their trust.

Rich, nourishing self-care is making sure that we communicate well with our parts. It means approaching our parts with curiosity and nonjudgment. It means acknowledging their feelings, understanding their needs, hearing their stories, and recognizing their role within our system of parts. It can be done; it just takes practice.

Rich, nourishing self-care is making sure that we communicate well with our parts. It means approaching our parts.

We have to learn to listen.

We must ask questions to our parts and listen to their answers from within. We must learn the practiced art of recognizing when our parts are speaking to us. My parts tend to communicate with me through visual imagery. They show me the things they are thinking or feeling, and when I close my eyes, I can see the images in front of me like a movie screen. Other people say that their parts communicate with them through intuitive feelings or body sensations. It can take time to learn how our parts communicate with us, and it's often made easier when done with the guidance of a therapist.

But if you're reading this book and not in a position to find a therapist at this time, let me give you a technique I learned in my own therapy sessions for accessing our parts. Imagine you're feeling really anxious, but you don't know why. You look around your environment and don't see anything that would cause this feeling. You are in no immediate danger; in fact, you're quite safe. It's likely that, in a moment like this, there is a part who is experiencing something that you don't have direct, conscious access to. That part of you is reliving a memory or a feeling you cannot see or feel. Or perhaps the part is perceiving something that you are too distracted to notice, but they notice because the trauma they carry has taught them to be hypervigilant.

When that happens, you can close your eyes, take a deep breath, and say to yourself, "I am here to listen to whatever part is seeking my attention. What are you worried about? And what do you need from me?" Your parts may be reluctant to confide in you at first, if it's your first time. They might be especially reluctant if you have ignored or invalidated them in the past. But with careful practice and determination, you will find your parts beginning to trust and confide in you. Same as when you reached out to the inner child that we talked about earlier.

Our parts, just like us, have a deep yearning to be heard. They want their feelings to be acknowledged, understood, and cared for. When we meet our parts' emotions with openness, curiosity, and compassion, we show them that they matter. We reassure them that we are listening. With time, our parts can let their guard down. They can see that we love and respect them, that we truly want the best for them. In turn, their self-esteem grows. They feel healthier, less afraid of the world, of the people in it, and most of all, of *us*. And when we are filled with parts who feel accepted and understood, when we embrace the diversity within ourselves, we cultivate a sense of wholeness and inner harmony. We become the kind of people who naturally communicate well with others, who find getting along with others a lot easier because we are comprised of many parts who *like who they are, who feel likable by others, and who have had good communication modeled to them over and over through the loving dialogue we give them.*

Self-care, my kind, gentle, unique, and multifaceted friend, is understanding that there are no bad parts.

No parts undeserving of love.

No parts unqualified to speak up.

No parts unworthy of reaching for what they deserve.

Each part of our beautiful selves is magnificent in its own sparkling way. Each deserves our utmost compassion and respect. Each deserves to be heard. When we do the difficult work of assimilating our parts into a healthier, happier self, we find a well of self-love, authenticity, and harmony with others comes bubbling to the surface.

As for that conversation with Charlie, we ended up having it later that evening when I had calmed down and returned to self. You might be wondering what we had discussed that had gotten one of my parts activated and pushed me out of self, but to be honest? I don't remember what it was.

That's kind of the beauty of choosing to put our conversations on pause until we are back in a state of self. It turns out that whatever had me upset enough to recognize that I wasn't in self was really no big deal at all. If this book has shown you anything, it's that I have an impeccable memory for details that matter to me. The fact that I can't remember what we were discussing at that time shows that it was a small thing, something unworthy of creating a scene over.

Self-care in our relationships, at the root of every human connection we have, is striving to communicate from self. It is choosing to show up in our relationships with others in a way that fosters mutual positive regard, trust, and goodwill. It means doing the same for our parts, too. When we choose to prioritize harmony with ourselves and with others, we find that the work of self-care is easy and light.

Self-care in our relationships, at the root of every human connection we have, is striving to communicate from self.

Self-care, after all, shouldn't bring us only to a deeper love of ourselves. It should bring us to a place of healing, of relationship, and of community—the kind that brings the true fulfillment that our souls will always long for.

The kind that knows how to reach for more than just potato chips.

Cultivate Your Truth Trench

- **There are no bad parts.** Take time to identify and name your internal parts. Explore the goals, priorities, and roles each one has in your overall well-being. Recognize that each part serves a purpose, and none are inherently bad. Some may need a little (or a lot) of attention and healing, but there are no bad parts.
- **You show up best for yourself and for others when you are in self.** Learn to recognize when you are in a state of self, where the goals and needs of all your parts come together in balance. The best way to tell if you are in self is if you experience calmness, curiosity, clarity, compassion, confidence, courage, creativity, and connectedness. When you are not feeling those things, there might be a part who is needing your attention.
- **All of your parts deserve love and guidance from you.** Speak to your parts (and yourself) with kindness, honesty, and compassion. Validate your feelings and acknowledge the needs of your internal parts. Cultivate a loving inner dialogue that fosters self-esteem and authenticity.
- **Listen to your parts and believe what they tell you.** Develop the skill of listening to your internal parts. Ask questions, observe visual imagery, or tune into intuitive feelings to understand their perspectives and needs. When you create a safe space for your parts to express themselves, you begin to develop internal harmony with your parts and external harmony with others.

Final Thoughts:

Self-Care in the Abyss

Write when your mental health is in the garbage. Edit when it's not.

This is the advice I've always given to people who write. Whether it's academic, scholarly, fiction, or nonfiction, I've always said to write when your mental health is poor. For me personally, and for most writers I know, our best and most effective writing in all forms comes when our mental health is in the shitter. So, I'm going to take a bit of my own advice and write to you from the abyss.

I'm currently sitting in my bed, exhausted, after throwing what I call a sensory tantrum. It's what I do when I have stuffed all my hard feelings so deep down that I can't get them out anymore. They're stuck way down there somewhere, and they're poisoning me from the inside. I can't make myself cry even though I want to. When this happens, I shut my bedroom door, climb into bed, and beat the absolute living hell out of my mattress. When I'm done, the tears finally come.

I'm not doing well today. It's going on three weeks of stuffing my feelings, pretending everything is okay so that I can keep functioning the way I need to.

Flirting with my husband.

Smiling at my kids.

Performing on social media.

Very diligently doing none of the things I've been preaching about in this book.

And I'm so tired of it.

These are the kinds of things you're not supposed to share when you're writing about self-care, right? You're supposed to show how healthy, strong, and balanced you are because of all that decadent self-care you've been doing. But I feel like I'd be a fraud if I didn't at least share this one moment with you. You need to know that even the best kind of self-care won't make you immune from moments like the one I'm having right now.

Some things have been going on in my life that feel totally out of my control. As a borderline control freak, type-A Capricorn, I think I hate feeling out of control most of all. It's starting to make me feel like I'm losing my grip. Lost in the abyss of all the things I can't control, I'm now watching myself falter even on the things I can control.

For example, I just lost it on my daughter for spilling my glass of water. I'm not really a yeller, so I didn't yell. My personal brand of "losing it" has a more avoidant flavor. I let out an exasperated sigh, bolted out of my chair, stormed to my bedroom, and shut the door. I'm pretty sure she was still following me when I closed it. It's possible I shut it right in her face.

Sometimes, I wish I would just yell.

It wasn't about the spill. It wasn't that anything was broken or stained. It wasn't about the goddamn water at all. It was that one more thing had gone wrong, one more thing happened that I couldn't control—the final, tiny thing that sent me to outer space.

I am so unproud of how I just acted. And yes, I am sticking with "unproud," and I'm just going to ignore the glaring red line underneath it screaming that's not a real word!

I know it's not a real word. It just happens to be the one that most accurately describes how I feel. I'm not ashamed of myself. I'm not embarrassed. I'm not feeling guilty, necessarily. At least by now in my self-care journey I've learned to accept that sometimes I will act in ways I don't like and that's because I'm human. It has to be okay.

So, it is okay. I'm not going to beat myself up about it, and in a few moments, after I've gathered myself, I'm going to apologize to my daughter. I'll at least use this moment to model sincere apology giving and humility. But right now, sitting here in the bed where I just beat the shit out of my own mattress, I feel unproud. I'm not proud of how I handled myself.

Fulfilling self-care, the kind that can nourish and heal, allows for several things to be true at once. It is knowing that you are allowed to be a work in progress. It is true that I have grown incredibly in my two-year journey of healing. It is also true that I am still super messed up and unhealed. My time here in the abyss doesn't erase the times I soar. The only self-care that is worth a damn is the kind that allows you to treat yourself gently, with self-compassion, even when you're doing the things that make you unproud.

Self-care understands that your mental health is real. It acknowledges that sometimes, your mental health can take away the sparkly bits of who you are. My mental health sometimes makes me anxious, prone to being tense and snippy with other people. Sometimes, my mental health makes me depressed. I can still get out of bed, still do my work, still take care of my kids. But I see the world as nothing but doom and gloom, robbed of all joy or happiness. Taking a bath or giving myself a facial isn't going to make me feel less anxious or depressed. And frankly, even the fulfilling self-care stuff that I've described in this book can't help me much in these moments. I can't self-confidence my way out of my anxiety. I can't communicate my way out of depression. Those things are just tools in my tool belt. In times like these, they are, at best, things that keep me from plunging all the way into despair. But they can't keep me from feeling the hard things. They can't stop me from acting in ways I'm unproud of.

Maybe one day in my journey they will be able to do that. I hope so. Self-care in the meantime means giving myself permission to be unproud but not ashamed. It means acknowledging my progress and all the ways I need to keep working. I can choose to be realistic about where I am on my journey without feeling hopelessness or despair. Most importantly, I can have these horrifically low mental health days (weeks or months, even) and still be a person who is worthy of all the goodness I deserve when my mental health is in a better place.

I am not a fraud or a hypocrite. I am not someone who doesn't practice what I preach. I'm a human being who feels. Who hurts. Whose inner child sometimes bubbles to the surface and acts in childish ways because she feels scared, vulnerable, or all alone. I can be gentle toward myself in those moments—gentle toward my present self and to that inner child. Self-care is loving her and me both enough to know that these behaviors I don't like are a cry for help, a symptom of something deeper that needs my attention. Self-care is approaching whatever that need is with curiosity, intention, and grace. It is asking myself, *Where is this behavior or feeling really coming from, and what can I do to meet that need in this moment?* rather than beating myself up about it. It is being faithful in meeting the deeper need, no matter how long it may take.

Nourishing self-care, the kind that's not of the potato chip variety, is taking it one day at a time. Wherever you are in your journey, however your mental health is doing today, be gracious toward yourself. Reject the tendency toward self-reproach and criticism that can feel masochistically satisfying in the moment but is so poisonous to your spirit. Also, reject the toxic self-care culture out there that gives you permission to be an unhealed, destructive version of yourself because "that's just who you are." You'll end up alienating yourself from the people you love, and in the long run, that's not self-care. Those people aren't doing you any favors with that message. Acknowledge that you are a work in progress. You are worthy and enough just as you are, but you deserve the kind of life that fills you up to the absolute brim. The kind of life that you feel proud of, that leads to deep, sincere self-love and an authentic love of those around you.

Some days, you may only have the energy for self-care potato chips: Maybe a bath or a facial, a trip to the grocery store without your kids, or taking a mental-health day from work is all you can muster. It's okay to let that be enough on those days. After all, there's nothing inherently wrong with potato chips: They feel good, they taste good. They require so much less effort than preparing a nutritious meal. They bring comfort. But as anyone who has ever binge eaten an entire bag of potato chips knows, those empty calories wear off fast. You quickly find yourself hungry again and have to eat something nourishing instead.

So, enjoy the self-care potato chips when that's all you can reach for. Just make sure you're reaching for the nourishing self-care, too. Speak your needs. Hold your boundaries. Give gentleness and firmness in equal measure, and always in the right context.

Take up space. Be heard. Be unapologetically you. Love yourself enough to insist on being treated the way you deserve. Love your people enough to do the hard work of healing and growth so that you treat them the way they deserve.

Speak your truth. Listen with intention. Try not to take things personally. Forgive others. More importantly, forgive yourself.

Know your worth when you're at the top of the mountain and when you are in the abyss. Give yourself grace when you make mistakes. Accept that it's a journey and that you've got a lifetime to get there. You can't hate yourself into the kind of nourishing, fulfilling, abundant life you deserve. So, know that it's okay to have setbacks and to make mistakes. Decide to get up and keep trying because you deserve to be nourished and fulfilled.

And when you're ready, put down the potato chips.

Acknowledgments

A woman filled with contradictions only thrives when surrounded by a diverse crowd of people—the ones who gently coax out the brilliant and shining things but can also wrestle the darker things back to the ground. And I've learned something from them all.

Charlie: You taught me how to be as soft as velvet but as strong as steel. There is no other person I'd rather have in my corner, in my kitchen, in my bed, or in my heart.

My son, Roman: You taught me how big my heart could expand, and what great capacity for love I possess. You made me a Mommy. From you, I inherited my most important role. Never forget that.

My daughter, Abby: You teach me every day what sincere happiness and joy look like. I want to be just like you one day, my little Caboosey. May you never forget to sparkle.

Mom and Dad: You taught me that love overcomes everything, outmatches everything, outlasts everything. You are the original cycle breakers of our family. You told me that all you could give me were *morals, manners,* and *an education*, and the rest was up to me. You've given me so much more than that. I promise to always stay in the light.

My Planeteer Friends: You know who you are. You taught me that I am worthy and deserving of love exactly as I am—that I can be perfect or I can be an absolute train wreck, and you'll love me just the same. To the one who's the *ride or die*, I love you the most.

My literary agent: Rachelle: You believed in me. You taught me to try believing in myself, too. I'll never forget hitting my knees in unrestrained jubilation the day I got your call.

My therapist who cannot be named: You were the first person to teach me not to reach for self-care potato chips. If there is any wisdom found in this book, it came directly from you.

There are people who I hope to continue to learn things from, whose impact on my life is just beginning. To my editor, Christine, thank you for turning the potato chips I gave you into something so much heartier. This book is radically better because you touched it, and I will never forget that. To the entire team at HCI and Simon & Schuster, thank you for your belief in me and for the passion you put into this project.

To my growing community of women who inspire me every day, thank you for being here. You mean so much more to me than you know. I must especially thank The Sensible Mama crew who have been there from the start. Of all the blessings I don't deserve, you are at the top.

And since I can't think of any better way to conclude this labor of love, I guess I'll do it the way I've always done it.

Love ya.

Mean it!

Always.

And I'll see you in the next one.

Recommended Reading

Darling reader, I've mentioned some books throughout these chapters that really helped me along my journey of self-care, healing, and personal growth. I would be honored if you would consider reading some (or all!) of them. Each one gave me something beautiful to cling to in the dark moments and something I recognize and celebrate when I found myself in the light. I hope they do the same for you.

How to Keep House While Drowning by KC Davis

Inner Bonding by Margaret Paul, PhD

The Art of Happiness by the Dalai Lama and Howard Cutler

The 4-Hour Work Week by Timothy Ferriss

The Courage to Be Disliked by Ichiro Kishimi and Fumitake Koga

The Four Agreements by Don Miguel Ruiz

The Gifts of Imperfection by Brene Brown

Untamed by Glennon Doyle

About the Author

Amber Wardell, PhD, is a cognitive psychologist, business owner, and author dedicated to helping women prioritize themselves and engage in meaningful self-care. Amber's expertise includes emotion and cognition, research design, and statistical modeling, and her research on cognitive, metacognitive, and emotional self-regulation has been published in top-tier peer-reviewed journals.

She is the wife of Charlie and mother to their two children, Roman and Abby. Amber's mission is to empower women to find nourishment and fulfillment in their various roles. Her journey of radical self-care transformed her life and relationships, leading to a thriving marriage and a more patient approach to motherhood.

She is a contributor to *Psychology Today* where she writes about compassionate and intersectional feminism, and in her free time she runs her own blog focused on marriage, motherhood, and mental health.

Amber and her family reside in Atlanta, Georgia.

Website: http://www.amberwardell.com

Psychology Today: www.psychologytoday.com/us/contributors/amber-wardell-phd

Find Amber on TikTok, Instagram, and YouTube as Sensible Amber